VISUAL QUICKSTART GUIDE

Quark XPress 3.1

FOR THE MACINTOSH

Elaine Weinmann

Peachpit Press

Visual QuickStart Guide
QuarkXPress for the Macintosh
Elaine Weinmann

Peachpit Press, Inc.
2414 Sixth Street
Berkeley, CA 94710
(510) 548-4393
(510) 548-5991 (fax)

ISBN: 0-938151-011-3

0 9 8 7 6 5 4 3 2

Printed and bound in the United States.

Dedication

To Peter Lourekas, artist, teacher, partner, and computer wizard, without whose love and support I would not have dreamed of writing this book.

Thank You.

To Bert and Richard Weinmann, for their nourishment.

To Pamela Wye, artist, writer, and editor par excellence.

To Quark, Inc., for continuing to redefine the standard for page layout software.

To Ted Nace and Peachpit Press, for giving me the freedom to write the book I wanted to write.

To Peter Lourekas, for his technical advice.

To Theodora, Christ, Harriet, Steve, Nia and David, for being there.

To my students who are brave enough to ask questions when they are confused.

And to Chester the kitten, without whom writing this book would have been a million times easier.

Table of Contents

Chapter 1: **The Basics — Read me First!**

Introduction..1

The QuarkXPress screen 2

Using the mouse 4

Terminology 4

Menus 5

Dialog boxes 10

The Tool palette 12

The Measurements palette...............................13

The Document Layout palette 14

Keyboard shortcuts 15

Balloon Help 16

Measurement Systems 16

Chapter 2: **The Way QuarkXPress Works** 17

Chapter 3: **Create a Document**

Launch QuarkXPress...19

Create a new file 20

Save a new file 22

Save an existing file 24

Revert to Saved 24

Duplicate a file 25

Modify a document's page size.........................26

Open a file...27

Close a file...28

Quit the application 28

Chapter 4: **Getting Around**

Change view sizes..29

Move through a document 31

Chapter 5: **Text Input**

Create a text box...35

Resize a text box 36

Delete a text box...37

Move a text box 37

Input text 38

Text Overflow 38

Highlight text..39

Delete text 40

The Clipboard..40

Frame a text box 42

Text inset 44

Rotate a text box 45

Layer text boxes 46

Wrap text around a box...................................48

Modify columns...49

Save Text 50

Chapter 6: **Text Flow**

Auto page insertion..51

Import text..52

Insert pages manually 54

Delete pages..57

Rearrange pages 58

Link text boxes..59

Unlink text boxes...60

Create jump lines 62

Chapter 7: **Paragraph Formatting**

Paragraph indents 63

Leading 66

Add space between paragraphs.........................68

Keep lines together...69

Insert a line break 70

Hanging indents 71

The Indent Here character................................72

Automatic drop caps.......................................73

Set tabs..75

Paragraph rules 80

Hyphenation..83

Apply an H&J 84

Chapter 8: **Typography**

Resize type..85

Change fonts..86

Style type 87

Horizontal alignment 88

Vertical alignment...89

Tracking and kerning.....................................90

Horizontal scaling 92

Baseline Shift...93

Insert special characters.................................94

Chapter 9: **Pictures**

Create a picture box 95

Resize a picture box..96

Delete a picture box 97

Move a picture box..97

Create a bleed 98

Use a guide to position a box........................99

Import a picture 100

Resize a picture 101

Crop a picture...103

Delete a picture..103

Convert a picture box shape 104

Rotate a picture 105

Frame a picture box.......................................107

Create a polygon..108

Reshape a polygon 109

Style a picture 110

Save a page as an EPS 112

Wrap text around a box................................114

Wrap text around a picture...........................115

Layer a picture behind text...........................118

Update a picture...119

Chapter 10: **Lines**

Draw a line...121

Style a line 122

Resize a line...123

Move a line 124

Chapter 11: **Style Sheets**

About style sheets 125

Create a style sheet 126

Apply a style sheet..128

The Based On option.......................................129

Edit a style sheet 130

Append style sheets 132

Duplicate a style sheet....................................134

Delete a style sheet 134

Chapter 12: **Master Pages**

About master pages...135

Automatic page numbering 136

Modify a master page..137

Create a master page...137

Rename a master page.......................................137

Apply a master page 138

Copy master items...139

Modify margin and column guides 139

Number sections..140

Chapter 13: **Color**

Create a spot color 141

Create a process color.......................................143

Edit a color 144

Apply color 145

Create a linear blend..147

Chapter 14: **Libraries**

Create a library 149

Open a library 150

Add or delete a library entry 151

Retrieve a library entry....................................153

Label a library entry 154

Chapter 15: **Multiple Items**

Group items..155

Modify grouped items.....................................156

Lock an item..157

Duplicate an item..158

Step and Repeat 159

Copy an item between documents 160

Align items...161

Distribute items 162

Layer items..163

Anchor a box...164

Chapter 16: **Search & Replace**

Check Spelling..165

Find/Change.. 170

Font Usage.. 172

Chapter 17: **Printing**...173

Chapter 18: **Default Settings** 175

Appendix A: **Glossary** 177

Appendix B: **List of Keyboard Shortcuts**............179

Index 185

THE BASICS 1

Introduction.

QuarkXPress is complex. That's why you bought a book. People rave about QuarkXPress because it's a great typesetting and layout tool and offers so many features for making documents, but having so many options can be daunting to a newcomer. The purpose of this Visual QuickStart Guide is to direct you down the main thoroughfares with step-by-step instructions and lots of illustrations. There are also many special tips to help you avoid getting "stuck."

This is a guidebook, and it is designed for page-flipping, complete with thumb tabs, though I recommend that you read Chapters 1 and 2 first. Like a visitor in a foreign country, give yourself time to get acquainted with the turf, where the various menus, features, screen icons, and commands are located, as well as with the QuarkXPress language.

Don't worry if you feel confused or clumsy at first. Remember how you felt the first time you tried to ride a bicycle or drive a car. With practice, many actions will become automatic, and you will have a powerful new tool at your disposal.

The QuarkXPress screen.

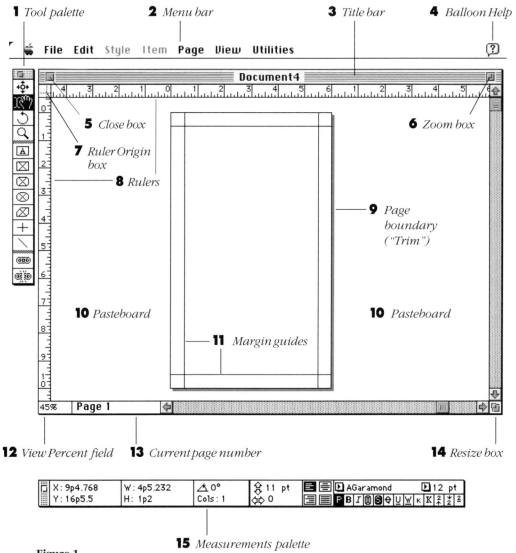

1 *Tool palette* **2** *Menu bar* **3** *Title bar* **4** *Balloon Help*

File   Edit   Style   Item   Page   View   Utilities

5 *Close box*

7 *Ruler Origin box*

8 *Rulers*

6 *Zoom box*

9 *Page boundary ("Trim")*

10 *Pasteboard* **10** *Pasteboard*

11 *Margin guides*

12 *View Percent field* **13** *Current page number* **14** *Resize box*

45% Page 1

X: 9p4.768   W: 4p5.232   ⊿ 0°   ⇧ 11 pt   AGaramond   12 pt
Y: 16p5.5   H: 1p2   Cols: 1   ⇔ 0   P B I ⓘ ⓢ ⓠ U W K K

15 *Measurements palette*

Figure 1.

The QuarkXPress Screen

Key to the QuarkXPress Screen.

1 *Tool palette*

There are seven moveable palettes. The Tools, Measurements, Document Layout, Style Sheets, Colors, and Trap Information palettes are opened from the View menu. Library palettes are opened from the Utilities menu.

2 *Menu bar*

Press any of the menu bar headings to access a list of dialog boxes, pop-up menus, commands and features.

3 *Title bar*

The file name is displayed in the document's title bar. Press and drag the title bar to move the document window.

4 *Balloon Help*

With Balloon Help on, moving the cursor over an item will open a small balloon containing information about that item. Turn Balloon Help on and off from the Help menu.

5 *Close box*

Click the Close box to close the currently active file.

6 *Zoom box*

Click the Zoom box to enlarge the document window; click on it again to return the window to its previous size. Clicking the Zoom box will force the screen to redraw.

7 *Ruler Origin box*

Press and drag from the ruler origin box to reposition the intersection of the horizontal and vertical rulers, also known as the zero point. Click on the ruler origin box to reset the zero point to the uppermost left corner of the page.

8 *Rulers*

Ruler increments can be displayed in one of seven measurement systems. Select Show Rulers or Hide Rulers from the View menu. Guides can be dragged from the vertical and horizontal rulers to aid in the layout process.

9 *Page boundary*

The edge, or "trim" size, of the page.

10 *Pasteboard*

Items can be created on the pasteboard and then dragged onto any document page, or stored on the pasteboard for later use.

11 *Margin Guides*

Margin guides are displayed for layout purposes only and do not print. Select Show Guides and Hide Guides from the View menu.

12 *View Percent field*

The view size of a document is displayed, and can be modified, in this field.

13 *Current Page number*

The number of the currently displayed page.

14 *Resize box*

Press and drag this box to resize the document window.

15 *Measurements palette*

Many of the commands that are listed under the various menus are accessible in the Measurements palette.

How to use the mouse:

The mouse is used in three basic ways.

Click

Press and release the mouse button quickly.

Use to: Select an item, activate a dialog box button, or create an insertion point in text.

Double-click

Press and release the mouse button twice in quick succession.

Use to: Launch an application, open or import a file, select a word, or highlight an entry field.

Press and drag

Press and hold down the mouse button, move the mouse on the mousepad, then release the mouse button.

Use to: Highlight text, select from a menu or pop-up menu, create or resize a box or line, or move an item, palette, or window.

Other terms used in this book:

Highlight

Select text by pressing and dragging over it or by clicking twice to select a word, three times to select a line, or four times to select a paragraph.
(See Chapter 5, Highlight Text)

Enter

A highlighted field.

A new value entered.

Completely highlight the contents of an entry field (referred to as "field"), on the Measurements palette or in a dialog box and replace with a new value. Double-clicking is sufficient to highlight most, but not all, fields. Press Tab to highlight the next field in succession. Press Shift-Tab to highlight the previous field. If more than one value exists within a selection in the document, the corresponding entry field will be blank. A new value can be entered into a blank box.

Check/Uncheck

Turn an option on or off by clicking the check box. A checked box indicates that an option is turned on.

Press

Quickly press and release a key on the keyboard.
(See Keyboard Shortcuts in this chapter)

Select

Choose from a menu or pop-up menu by pressing and dragging to highlight a selection, then releasing the mouse button, or click once on an item so that it can be modified.
(See Menus on the following page)

Using the Mouse; Terminology

How to use a menu.

Press and drag from a menu heading downward and release the mouse button when a selection is highlighted. Select from a pop-up menu by pressing and dragging downward through the main menu and then to the right or left through the pop-up menu. Release the mouse when a selection is highlighted.

About menus:

Each of the seven menu headings provides access to related commands for modifying layouts and page elements and executing various functions. The seven menus are illustrated on the following pages.

Figure 2.

Keyboard equivalents for some menu commands are listed using the following symbols:

⌘ = Command key
⇧ = Shift key

Selecting a menu item that is followed by an ellipsis (...) opens a dialog box.

A dotted line separates commands that are grouped into sub-categories.

Menu items that are dimmed are temporarily unavailable.

A check mark indicates that a command is turned on.

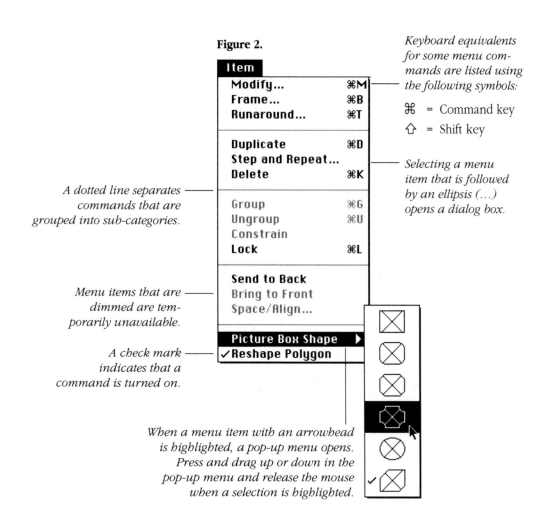

When a menu item with an arrowhead is highlighted, a pop-up menu opens. Press and drag up or down in the pop-up menu and release the mouse when a selection is highlighted.

Menus

The File menu.

Most File menu commands apply to the document as a whole, such as creating, opening, closing, saving, or printing a file. Other File menu commands include exporting text, importing text and pictures, and quitting the application.

The Edit menu.

Edit menu commands include Select All, Clear, Preferences, Clipboard functions, Find/Change, Style Sheets, Colors and H&Js. The Undo command will undo the last modification made.

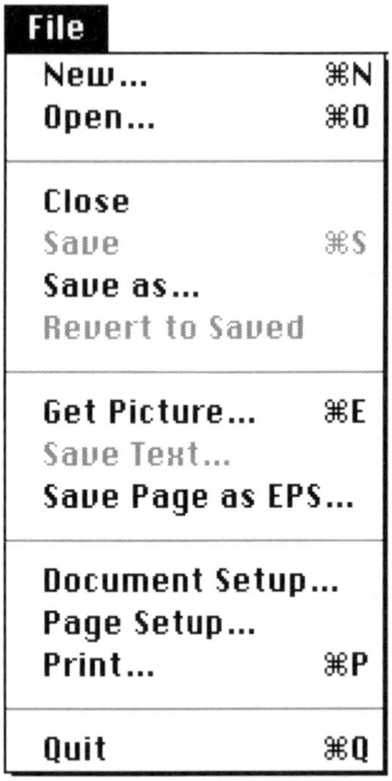

File	
New...	⌘N
Open...	⌘O
Close	
Save	⌘S
Save as...	
Revert to Saved	
Get Picture...	⌘E
Save Text...	
Save Page as EPS...	
Document Setup...	
Page Setup...	
Print...	⌘P
Quit	⌘Q

Figure 3. *The File menu.*

Edit	
Undo Item Change	⌘Z
Cut	⌘X
Copy	⌘C
Paste	⌘V
Clear	
Select All	⌘A
Subscribe To...	
Subscriber Options...	
Show Clipboard	
Find/Change	⌘F
Preferences	▶
Style Sheets...	
Colors...	
H&Js...	

Figure 4. *The Edit menu.*

The Style menu.

Style menu commands modify the contents of a text box, including typographic specifications and paragraph formatting, when text is selected; they modify the contents of a picture box, such as color, shade or contrast, when a picture is selected; they modify line attributes when a line is selected. The Style menu is available only when the Content tool and an item are selected.

Style

Font	▶
Size	▶
Type Style	▶
Color	▶
Shade	▶
Horizontal Scale...	
Track...	
Baseline Shift...	
Character...	⌘⇧D
Alignment	▶
Leading...	⌘⇧E
Formats...	⌘⇧F
Rules...	⌘⇧N
Tabs...	⌘⇧T
Style Sheets	▶

Figure 5. *The Style menu with a **text box** selected.*

Style

Line Style	▶
Endcaps	▶
Width	▶
Color	▶
Shade	▶

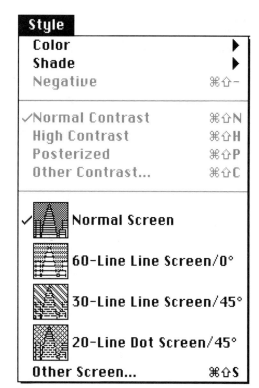

Style

Color	▶
Shade	▶
Negative	⌘⇧-
✓Normal Contrast	⌘⇧N
High Contrast	⌘⇧H
Posterized	⌘⇧P
Other Contrast...	⌘⇧C
✓ Normal Screen	
60-Line Line Screen/0°	
30-Line Line Screen/45°	
20-Line Dot Screen/45°	
Other Screen...	⌘⇧S

Figure 7. *The Style menu with a **picture box** selected.*

Figure 6. *The Style menu with a **line** selected.*

The Item menu.

Item menu commands modify items — text boxes, pictures boxes, and lines. Deleting, framing, grouping, duplicating, locking, aligning and layering are some Item commands. The Item menu is available only when an item is selected.

The Page menu.

Page menu commands are used to add, delete and number pages, move through a document, and modify master guides.

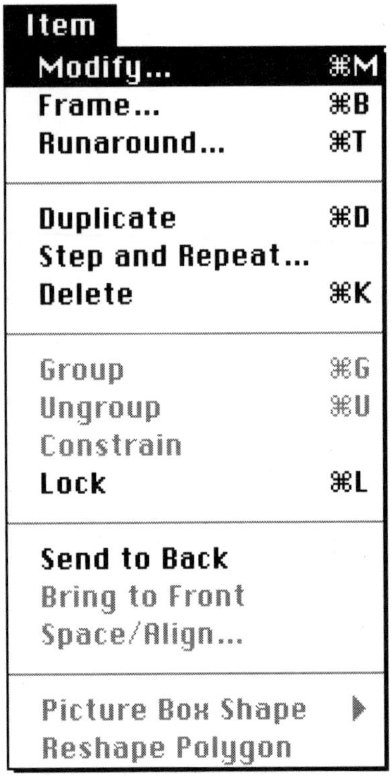

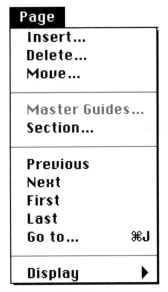

Figure 8. *The Item menu.*

Figure 9. *The Page menu.*

The View menu.

View menu commands control document view sizes and the display of guides, rulers, invisibles and palettes.

The Utilities menu.

Utilities menu commands include miscellaneous functions, such as checking spelling, libraries, picture and font usage, tracking and kerning tables, and optional XTensions.

View	
Fit in Window	⌘0
50%	
75%	
Actual Size	⌘1
200%	
Thumbnails	
Hide Guides	
Show Baseline Grid	
Snap to Guides	
Hide Rulers	⌘R
Show Invisibles	⌘I
Hide Tools	
Hide Measurements	
Show Document Layout	
Show Style Sheets	
Show Colors	
Show Trap Information	
Show Value Converter	
Windows	▶

Figure 10. *The View menu.*

Utilities	
Check Spelling	▶
Auxiliary Dictionary...	
Edit Auxiliary...	
Suggested Hyphenation...	⌘H
Hyphenation Exceptions...	
Library...	
Font Usage...	
Picture Usage...	
Tracking Edit...	
Kerning Table Edit...	
Remove Manual Kerning	
Alternate Em Spaces	

Figure 11. *The Utilities menu.*

Dialog boxes:

Dialog boxes are like fill-in forms with multiple choices. The various methods of indicating one's choices are shown in **Figures 12-14**. Click OK or press Return to exit a dialog box and implement the indicated changes.

Dialog boxes can be opened from menus or through keyboard shortcuts. A dialog box will open when any menu item that is followed by an ellipsis (...) is selected.

✔ Tips

- In any dialog box, press Tab to highlight the next field. Hold down Shift and press Tab to highlight the previous field.
- Hold down Command (⌘) and press "Z" to undo changes made in a dialog box since it was opened.

*Round **buttons** can be clicked on and off. Only one button can be selected per group.*

*Numbers can be typed into **fields** in any of the seven measurement systems used in QuarkXPress.*

***Check box** options can be clicked on or off. If there is an "x" in a check box, that option is turned on.*

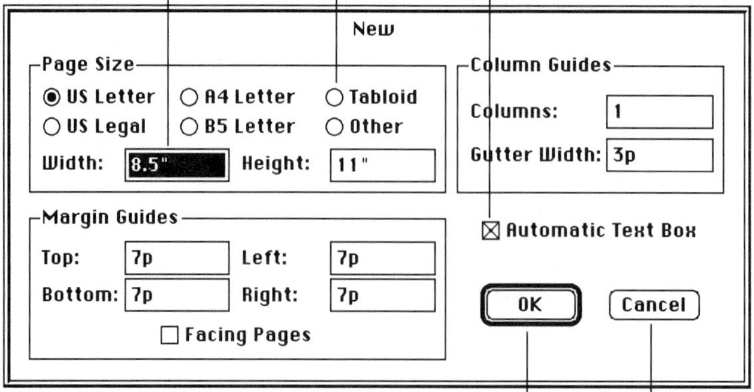

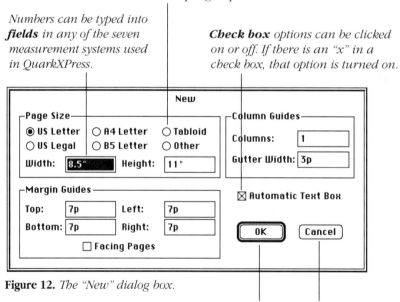

Figure 12. *The "New" dialog box.*

*Click **OK** or press **Return** on the keyboard to exit a box and accept the new settings.*

*Click **Cancel** to exit a box with no modifications taking effect.*

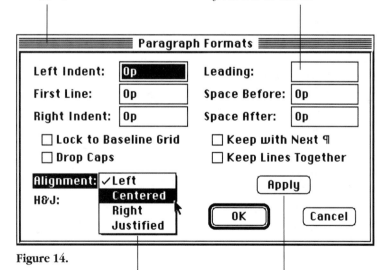

Figure 13.
Boxes with shadows open into pop-up menus.

Some dialog boxes can be moved by pressing and dragging their title bars.

If more than one value exists within a selection in the document, the corresponding field will be blank. For example, if highlighted text includes 8 pt. and 12 pt. leading, the Leading field will be blank.

Figure 14.

Press and drag the mouse to make a selection from a pop-up menu.

*Click **Apply** or hold down Command (⌘) and press "A" to preview modifications in the document with the dialog box open. Hold down **Option** and click **Apply** to turn on Continuous Apply mode. Hold down Option and click Apply again to turn off Continuous apply mode.*

Dialog Boxes

The Tool palette.

The Tool palette contains 13 tools for editing, item creation, and linking. Like all palettes, the Tool palette is moved by pressing and dragging the dotted bar, and closed by clicking the Close box. The Tool palette is opened or closed by selecting Show Tools or Hide Tools from the View menu.

✔ Tips

■ To select the next tool in the Tool palette using the keyboard, hold down Command (⌘) and press Tab. To select the previous tool, hold down Command (⌘) and Shift and press Tab.

■ Hold down Option and select any item creation or linking tool to keep it selected. To deselect a tool, click on another tool.

Figure 15.
The Tool palette.

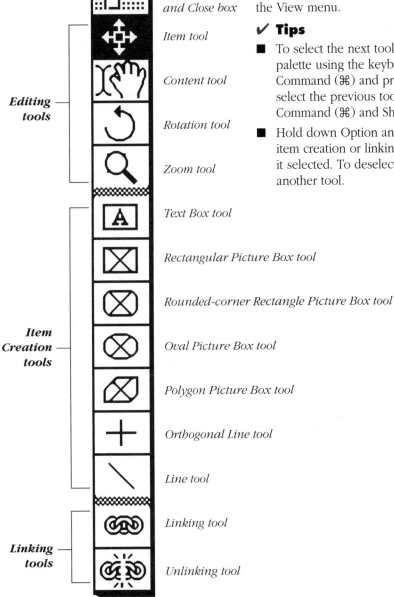

Dotted bar
and Close box

Item tool

Content tool

Rotation tool

Zoom tool

Editing tools

Text Box tool

Rectangular Picture Box tool

Rounded-corner Rectangle Picture Box tool

Oval Picture Box tool

Polygon Picture Box tool

Orthogonal Line tool

Line tool

Item Creation tools

Linking tool

Unlinking tool

Linking tools

The Tool Palette

The Measurements palette.

The Measurements palette contains some of the commands and options that are available under menus. The information on the Measurements palette changes depending on what kind of item and tool are selected. The palette is blank when no item is selected. Appendix B lists keyboard shortcuts for use with the Measurements palette.

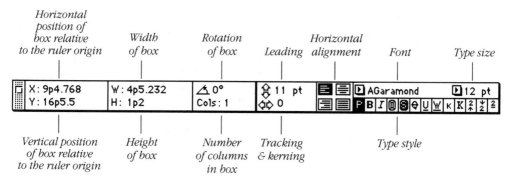

Figure 16. *The Measurements palette with the **Content tool** and a **text box** selected.*

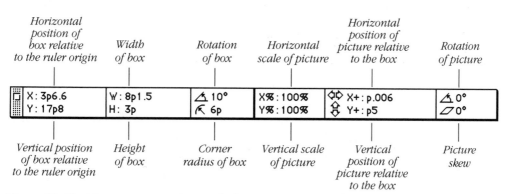

Figure 17. *The Measurements palette with the **Content tool** and a **picture box** selected.*

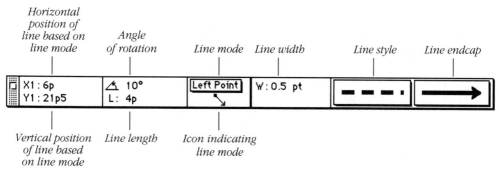

Figure 18. *The Measurements palette with the **Content tool** and a **line** selected.*

The Document Layout palette.

The Document Layout palette is used for rearranging pages, inserting and deleting pages, moving through a document, and creating, editing, and applying master pages.

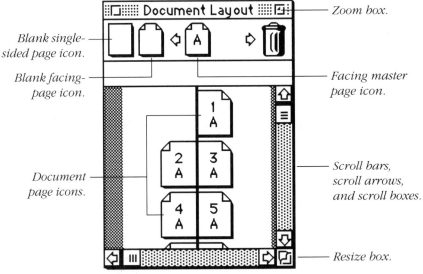

Zoom box.

Blank single-sided page icon.

Blank facing-page icon.

Facing master page icon.

Document page icons.

Scroll bars, scroll arrows, and scroll boxes.

Resize box.

Figure 19. *The Document Layout palette of a **facing-page** document.*

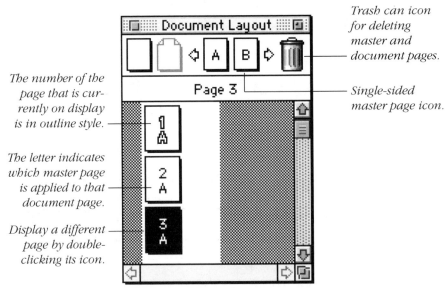

Trash can icon for deleting master and document pages.

The number of the page that is currently on display is in outline style.

Single-sided master page icon.

The letter indicates which master page is applied to that document page.

Display a different page by double-clicking its icon.

Figure 20. *The Document Layout palette of a **single-sided** document.*

The Document Layout palette

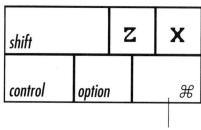

The Command key.

Figure 21. *The **Command** (⌘), **Option, Shift,** and **Control** keys are available on the left side of all Apple keyboards, and on the right side of an Apple extended keyboard.*

About keyboard shortcuts:

There are keyboard equivalents for many of the commands that are used in QuarkXPress. Most keyboard shortcuts are performed by holding down one or more keys on the keyboard, pressing and releasing another key or keys, and then finally releasing the first set of keys. For example, to perform the Save keystroke, hold down Command (⌘), press and release "S", then release Command.

(See Appendix B for a list of shortcuts)

To perform a keyboard shortcut:

1. Hold down the Command (⌘), Shift, Control, Option key or keys **(Figures 21-22)**.

2. Press and release the second key or keys.

3. Release the Command (⌘), Shift, Control, Option key or keys.

In this book, the Shift, Control, and Option keys are referred to by name. The Command name and icon (⌘) are used together to avoid confusion because the word "Command" does not appear on most keyboards.

✔ Tip

■ Do not use Enter in place of Return.

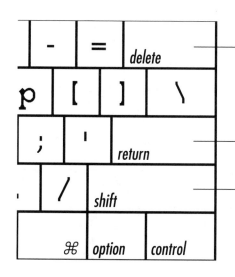

The **Delete** *key is used to delete text as well as text boxes, picture boxes, and lines.*

The **Return** *key is used to create new paragraphs. It is also used in lieu of pressing OK to exit a dialog box, or to accept changes made in the Measurements palette.*

The **Shift** *key is often used in keyboard shortcuts, but also maintains its traditional function for inputting uppercase characters.*

Figure 22. *The right side of an Apple extended keyboard.*

About Balloon Help:

If you are working on a computer that is operating with System 7 or later, a feature called Balloon Help is available. When this option is turned on and the cursor is moved over a screen icon, menu command, or dialog box, a balloon will open containing a brief description of that feature.

To turn Help Balloons on, select Show Balloons from the Help menu **(Figure 23)**.

To turn Help Balloons off, select Hide Balloons from the Help menu **(Figure 24)**.

Figure 23. *Select Show Balloons from the Help menu.*

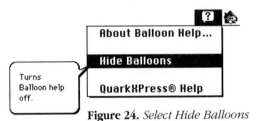

Figure 24. *Select Hide Balloons from the Help menu.*

About QuarkXPress' measurement systems:

Numbers in fields are displayed in the current default measurement system, but numbers can be entered in any of the other measurement systems used in QuarkXPress. The following measurement systems can be selected for a file: inches, inches decimal, picas, points, millimeters, centimeters, and ciceros **(Figures 25-26)**.

(See Chapter 18, Set Defaults)

✔ Tips

■ Do not enter "pts" for points or "in" for inches.

■ Picas and points can be combined. For example, to indicate four picas and six points, enter "4p6."

The seven measurement systems used in QuarkXPress. Use only these abbreviations in entry fields.	
Inches/ Inches Decimal	"
Picas	P
Points	pt
	or
	p followed by a number ("p6")
Centimeters	cm
Millimeters	mm
Ciceros	c

Figure 25. *Enter a number in any measurement system used in QuarkXPress.*

Figure 26. *When the Return key is pressed, the number is converted into the file's current default measurement system.*

THE WAY QUARKXPRESS WORKS

Figure 1. *A picture in a picture box. This box has a .25 point frame applied to it.*

Figure 2. *A picture box with no frame applied to it.*

"Beauty! I've starved myself since you forgot about me. Now at least I shall die in peace..."

"Live!" cried Beauty. "And let us marry. How could I live without you, my dearest Beast?"

Figure 3. *A text box with a frame.*

Figure 4. *A 2 point line.*

Like every software application, QuarkXPress has its own unique structure.

■ **Pictures and text must be placed in picture and text boxes. Lines are drawn independently.**

The border of a text or picture box will print only when a frame is applied to it **(Figures 1-4)**.

■ **Picture boxes, text boxes, and lines are defined as items.**

■ **The picture or text that is contained in a box is defined as the contents of the box.**

■ **To modify an item or its contents, the correct tool must be used.**

As a general rule, the Item tool is used to modify a box (an item), and the Content tool is used to modify the contents of a box (a picture or text). Tool selection is indicated as the first step for most procedures in this book. In some instances, the Item and Content tools can be used interchangeably, and this is also noted.

Click on a tool icon once to select a tool **(Figures 5-6)**.

Figure 5. *The **Item** tool.*

Figure 6. *The **Content** tool.*

- **An item must be selected before it can be modified (Figures 7-8).**

- **The information on the Measurements palette varies depending on which kind of tool and item is selected.**

  The left side of the Measurements palette will display item information pertaining to a picture box, text box, line, or group, such as its angle of rotation or position on the page, if it is selected with the Item or Content tool **(Figure 9a)**.

  The right side of the Measurements palette will display content information about a picture or text, such as point size or leading, only if it is selected with the Content tool **(Figures 9b)**. The right side of the Measurements palette will display information pertaining to the style of a line if it is selected with the Item or Content tool.

  The Measurements palette will be blank if no item is selected **(Figure 9c)**.

Figure 7. *A picture box that is not selected.*

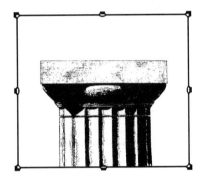

Figure 8. *Eight handles are displayed when a box is selected.*

	X : 21p10.425	W : 15p11.628	⌔ 0°	
	Y : 3p.887	H : 34p11.113	Cols : 1	

Figure 9a. *The Measurements palette with the **Item tool** and a **text box** selected.*

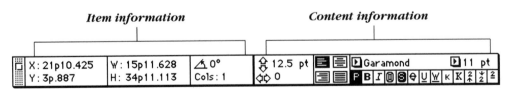

Item information   Content information

Figure 9b. *The Measurements palette with the **Content tool** and **text** selected.*

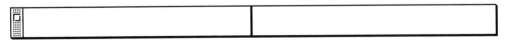

Figure 9c. *The Measurements palette with **no item** selected.*

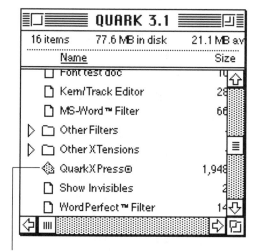

Figure 1. *Double-click the diamond-shaped application icon in the QuarkXPress folder.*

To launch QuarkXPress:

Double-click the QuarkXPress folder icon on the Finder desktop. Then double-click the diamond-shaped QuarkXPress application icon **(Figure 1)**.

or

Double-click any existing QuarkXPress file icon on the Finder desktop **(Figure 2)**.

✔ Tip

■ On a Macintosh with System 7 or later, the Finder desktop is visible at all times. If you activate the Finder desktop by accidentally clicking on it, return to QuarkXPress by clicking anywhere in an open QuarkXPress document window, or select QuarkXPress from the applications menu in the upper right-hand corner of the screen **(Figure 3)**.

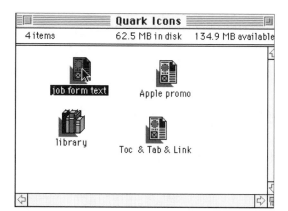

Figure 2. *Double-click any QuarkXPress file icon to launch the application **and** open the file simultaneously.*

Figure 3. *Select any open application from the applications menu.*

Launch QuarkXPress

To create a new file:

1. Launch QuarkXPress.
   (See instructions on previous page)

2. Select New from the File menu
   (Figure 4).

Steps 3-8 are optional.

3. Select a preset size by clicking one of
   the Page Size buttons **(Figure 5)**.
   or
   Enter numbers in the Width and Height
   fields to create a custom size document.

4. Check or uncheck the Facing Pages
   box.

5. Modify the numbers in the Margin
   Guides fields.

6. Modify the number of Columns.

7. Modify the number in the Gutter Width
   field if the number of columns is
   greater than 1.

8. Check the Automatic Text Box box
   to have a text box to appear automatically within the margin guides on every
   page in your document.

9. Click OK or press Return.

✔ Tips

■ Laser printers do not print to the edge
   of the paper. Enter margin guides of
   approximately ½" (3p) on an 8½" x 11"
   document.

■ If the page width of your document is
   greater than the page height, select the
   landscape Orientation icon in the Page
   Setup dialog box, opened from the File
   menu, before printing.
   (See Chapter 17, Printing)

■ Don't confuse the New dialog box,
   where new files are created, with the
   Open dialog box, which opens already
   existing files.

File	
New...	⌘N
Open...	⌘O
Close	
Save	⌘S
Save as...	
Revert to Saved	
Get Text...	⌘E
Save Text...	
Save Page as EPS...	
Document Setup...	
Page Setup...	
Print...	⌘P
Quit	⌘Q

Figure 4. *Select **New**
from the **File** menu.*

Figure 5. *The **New** dialog box.*

*Select a preset **Page Size** or enter custom numbers between 1" and 48" in the **Width** and **Height** fields. A4 Letter is 210 mm x 297 mm; B5 Letter is 182 mm x 257 mm; Tabloid is 11" x 17". Numbers in the Width and Height fields are always converted to inches, though they can be entered in any of the other measurement systems used in Quark XPress.*

*Enter a **Gutter Width** between 3 and 288 points (4").*

*Enter a number between 1 and 30 in the **Columns** field.*

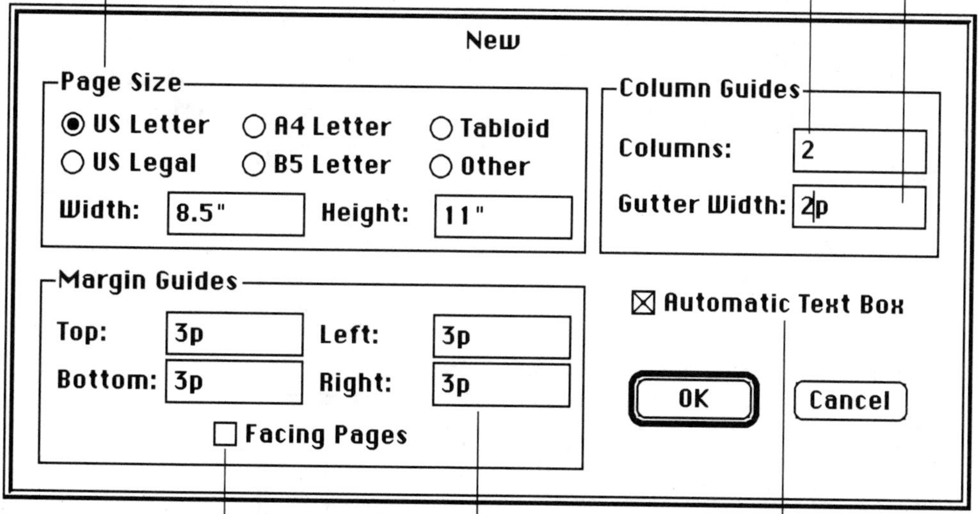

```
                          New

  ┌─Page Size────────────────────┐   ┌─Column Guides──────────┐
  │  ● US Letter   ○ A4 Letter   ○ Tabloid │                        │
  │  ○ US Legal    ○ B5 Letter   ○ Other   │  Columns:      [2    ] │
  │  Width: [8.5" ]   Height: [11" ]       │  Gutter Width: [2p   ] │
  └───────────────────────────────┘   └────────────────────────┘

  ┌─Margin Guides────────────────┐     ☒ Automatic Text Box
  │  Top:    [3p]   Left:  [3p]   │
  │  Bottom: [3p]   Right: [3p]   │       ( OK )    ( Cancel )
  │        □ Facing Pages         │
  └───────────────────────────────┘
```

*If you are creating a multiple-page document, such as a book, and want the first page to start by itself on the right-hand side with the remaining pages arranged side by side in pairs, check the **Facing Pages** box.*

*With the **Automatic Text Box** option checked, a text box containing the number of columns and gutter width specified in the Column Guides fields will appear on every page.*

*Margin Guides do not print, but are helpful in the layout process. When the Facing Pages box is checked, the Left and Right Margin Guides fields are converted to **Inside** and **Outside**.*

To save a new file:

1. Select Save from the File menu **(Figure 6)**.

2. The "Save current document as" field will be highlighted automatically. Type a document name **(Figure 7a)**.

3. If you are working on a Macintosh with System 6.07 or earlier, click Drive to select a location for the new file.

If you are working on a Macintosh with System 7 or later, click Desktop, select a drive from the scroll list, then click Open **(Figures 7b)**.

4. *Optional:* Select a folder or sub-folder in which to save the file, then Click Open.

5. Click Save **(Figure 7c)**.

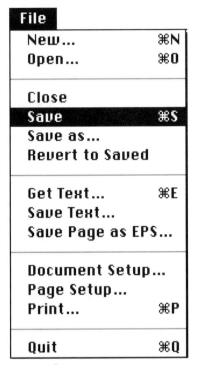

Figure 6. *Select* **Save** *from the* **File** *menu.*

Figure 7a. *The* **Save As** *dialog box with System 7 or later.*

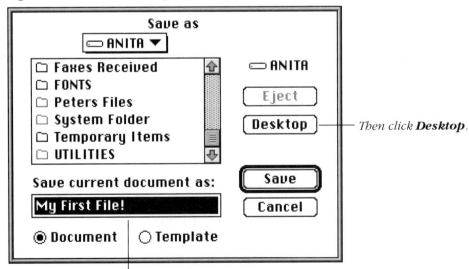

Then click **Desktop**.

First, type in a name for the new file in the **Save current document as** *field.*

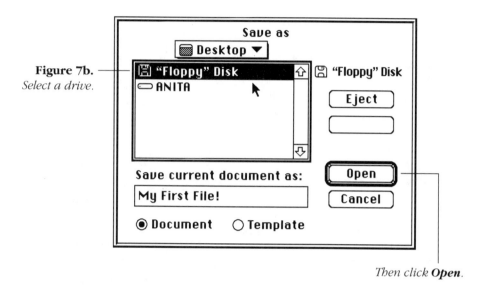

Figure 7b.
Select a drive.

*Then click **Open**.*

Figure 7c. *Make sure the name of
the disk or folder you have selected
to save in is displayed here.*

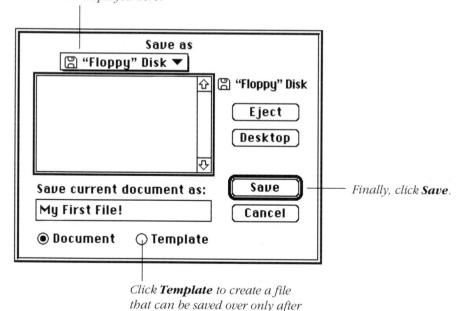

*Finally, click **Save**.*

*Click **Template** to create a file
that can be saved over only after
responding to a warning prompt.*

To save over an existing file:

Select Save from the File menu **(Figure 8)**.

or

Hold down Command (⌘) and press "S".

✔ Tips

■ **Save frequently!** You will be protected from machine "bombs" and will be able to take full advantage of the Revert to Saved feature.

■ The Save command under the File menu is dimmed when a file has been saved and no new modifications have been made to it.

To revert to the last saved version:

1. Select Revert to Saved from the File menu.

2. After the prompt "Revert to the last version saved?" appears, click OK or press Return **(Figure 9)**.

✔ Tip

■ The Revert to Saved feature can be used to return to an earlier version of a file while experimenting with multiple design variations, or to restore a file that has been modified by a household pet walking across your keyboard.

File

New...	⌘N
Open...	⌘O
Close	
Save	**⌘S**
Save as...	
Revert to Saved	
Get Text...	⌘E
Save Text...	
Save Page as EPS...	
Document Setup...	
Page Setup...	
Print...	⌘P
Quit	⌘Q

Figure 8. *Select **Save** from the **File** menu.*

Figure 9. *Selecting **Revert to Saved** from the **File** menu will cause this prompt to appear. Click OK to restore the last saved version.*

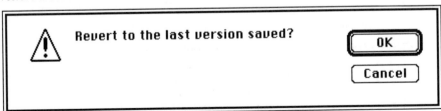

⚠ **Revert to the last version saved?**   [OK]
                                          [Cancel]

Save an Existing File; Revert to Saved

Figure 10. *Select **Save As** from the **File** menu.*

To duplicate a file:

1. Open a file to be duplicated.
2. Select Save As from the File menu **(Figure 10)**.
3. Enter a new name in the Save current document as field, or modify the existing name **(Figure 11)**.
4. Select a location in which to save the duplicate file.
5. Click Save.

✔ Tip

■ If the title of the active file is **not** altered in the Save as dialog box and you click Save, a warning prompt will appear. Click Replace to save over the original file, or click Cancel. The active file will not be duplicated.

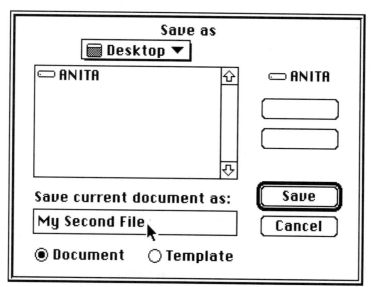

Figure 11. *Enter a new name for the duplicate file or alter the existing name, then click **Save**.*

To modify a document's page size:

1. Select Document Setup from the File menu **(Figure 12)**.

2. Click a preset page size.
or
Enter custom numbers in the Width and Height fields **(Figure 13)**.

3. Click OK or press Return.

✔ Tips

■ A single-sided document can be converted into a facing-page document by checking the Facing Pages box. To convert a facing-page document into a single-sided document, delete all the facing master pages in the document, and then uncheck the Facing Pages box.
(See Chapter 12, About Master Pages)

■ Column and margin guides are modified in the Master Guides dialog box, which can be opened from the Page menu when a master page is displayed.
(See Chapter 12, Modify Guides)

■ Reduced page size values will not be accepted if any items in the current file are too large to fit within the new pasteboard dimensions.

File

New...	⌘N
Open...	⌘O
Close	
Save	⌘S
Save as...	
Revert to Saved	
Get Picture...	⌘E
Save Text...	
Save Page as EPS...	
Document Setup...	
Page Setup...	
Print...	⌘P
Quit	⌘Q

Figure 12. *Select **Document Setup** from the **File** menu.*

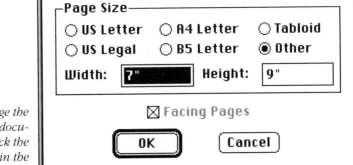

Figure 13. *Change the **Width** and **Height** of a document and check or uncheck the **Facing Pages** option in the Document Setup dialog box.*

Document Setup
Page Size
○ US Letter ○ A4 Letter ○ Tabloid
○ US Legal ○ B5 Letter ● Other
Width: 7" Height: 9"
☒ Facing Pages
OK Cancel

File	
New...	⌘N
Open...	⌘O
Close	
Save	⌘S
Save as...	
Revert to Saved	
Get Text...	⌘E
Save Text...	
Save Page as EPS...	
Document Setup...	
Page Setup...	
Print...	⌘P
Quit	⌘Q

Figure 14. *Select **Open** from the **File** menu to open an existing file.*

To open a QuarkXPress file from within the application:

1. Select Open from the File menu **(Figure 14)**.

2. Double-click a file name.
or
Click a file name once, then click Open. Up to seven QuarkXPress files can be open at a time **(Figure 16)**.

To open a QuarkXPress file from the Desktop:

Double-click the file icon. If the application has not yet been launched, double-clicking a QuarkXPress file will open the file and launch the application simultaneously **(Figure 15)**.

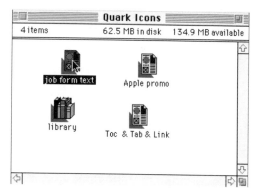

Figure 15. *Open a QuarkXPress file from the desktop by double-clicking the file icon.*

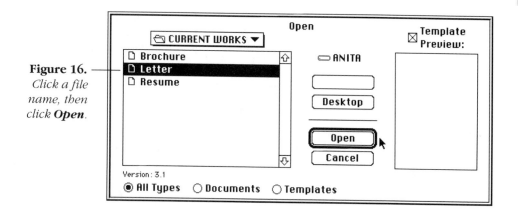

Figure 16. *Click a file name, then click **Open**.*

Open a File

To close a file:

Click the Close box in the upper left-hand corner of the document window **(Figure 17)**.

or

Select Close from the File menu.

✔ Tip

- If you attempt to close a file that has never been saved, a prompt will appear giving you the option to save or discard the file, or cancel the close operation **(Figure 19)**.

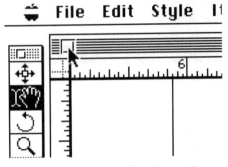

Figure 17. *Click the Close box in the upper left-hand corner of the document window to close a file.*

To quit the application:

Select Quit from the File menu **(Figure 18)**.

or

Hold down Command (⌘) and press "Q".

✔ Tip

- Quitting the application will close all open QuarkXPress files. If changes have been made to an open file since it was last saved, a prompt will appear giving you the option to save again before quitting or cancel the quit operation **(Figure 20)**.

Figure 18. *Select **Quit** from the **File** menu to close the application and close any open QuarkXPress files.*

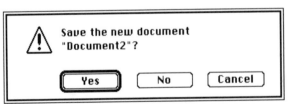

Figure 19. *If you attempt to close a file that has never been saved, this prompt will appear.*

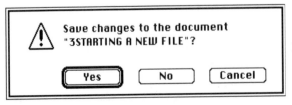

Figure 20. *If you attempt to quit the application and modifications were made to the file since it was last saved, this prompt will appear.*

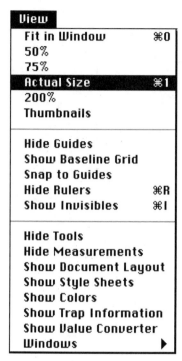

Figure 1. *Select from a list of view sizes under the **View** menu.*

There are many ways to move from page to page and to change from small to large display sizes, or "views." Modifying the view size of a file does not alter the actual page size, only the size at which it is displayed.

To select a view size from the View menu:

Select Fit in Window, 50%, 75%, Actual Size, 200%, or Thumbnails from the View menu **(Figure 1)**.

✔ Tip

■ Page elements cannot be modified in Thumbnails view. Pages within a file can be rearranged in Thumbnails view, and pages can be drag-copied from one file to another if both documents are in Thumbnails view. *(See Chapter 6, Rearrange Pages)*

To change the view size using the View Percent field:

1. Double-click in the View Percent field in the lower left-hand corner of the document window **(Figure 2)**.

2. Enter a number between 10 and 400.

3. Press Return.

✔ Tips

■ If the view size is changed when an item is selected or text is highlighted, the item or text will be centered in the document window in the new view size.

■ It is not necessary to enter the % symbol in the View Percent field.

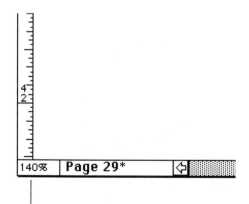

Figure 2. *The **View Percent field**.*

Change View Sizes

To change the view size using the Zoom tool from the keyboard:

Hold down Control and click on the page to enlarge the view size **(Figure 3)**.

or

Hold down Control and Option and click on the page to reduce the view size **(Figure 4)**.

or

Hold down Control and press and drag a marquee around an area on the page that you wish to enlarge **(Figure 5)**.

✔ Tip

■ Accessing the Zoom tool from the keyboard is faster than selecting and then deselecting the Zoom tool from the Tool palette.

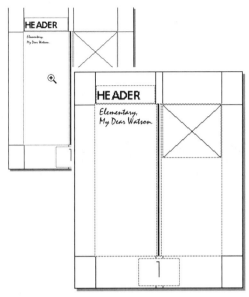

Figure 3. *Hold down **Control** and click on the page to enlarge the view size.*

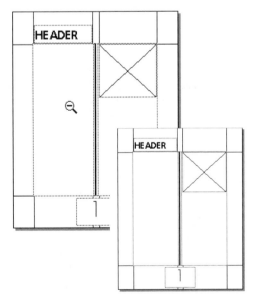

Figure 4. *Hold down **Option** and **Control** and click on a page to reduce the view size.*

Figure 5. *Hold down **Control** and press and drag over a section of a page to magnify that chosen area.*

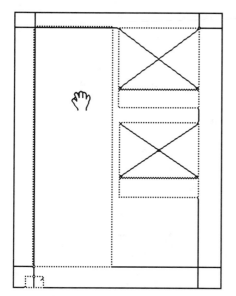

Figure 6. *Hold down* **Option** *and press and drag with the mouse to move a page in the document window.*

To move through a document using the page grabber hand:

Hold down Option and press and drag to move a page in the document window. The cursor will temporarily turn into a hand icon **(Figure 6)**.

✔ Tip

■ The Page Grabber Hand feature is turned on in the Application Preferences dialog box, opened from the Preferences pop-up menu under the Edit menu.

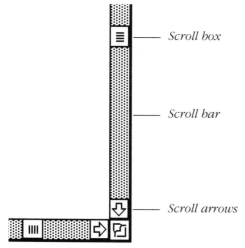

Figure 7. *The standard Macintosh window features: scroll boxes, bars, and arrows.*

Scroll box

Scroll bar

Scroll arrows

To move through a document using the scroll arrows, bars and boxes:

Click on a **scroll arrow** to move a short distance within a document in the direction the arrow is pointing **(Figure 7)**.
or
Move a **scroll box** to move through a document more quickly.
or
Click on a grey **scroll bar** to move through a document a full screen at a time. Click in the gray area above the scroll box to move a full screen upward, and below the box to move a full screen downward. Click to the left of the scroll box to move a full screen to the left, and to the right of the scroll box to move a full screen to the right.

To move through a document using an extended keyboard:

Press Page Up or Page Down to move up or down a full screen **(Figure 8)**.

or

Press Home to move to the beginning of a document or press End to move to the end of a document.

✔ Tip

■ Hold down Shift and press Page Up to display the top of the previous page, or Page Down to display the top of the next page.

Figure 8. *A section of an extended keyboard.*

To move through a document using the Page menu:

Select Previous, Next, First, or Last from the Page menu **(Figure 9)**.

or

Select Go to from the Page menu or hold down Command (⌘) and press "J". Enter the desired page number in the Go to Page field, then click OK or press Return **(Figure 10)**.

✔ Tip

■ If a page has a prefix applied using the Section command, be sure to enter the prefix before the number in the Go to dialog box. To display a page based on its position in the document rather than its applied Section number, enter "+" before the number.

(See Chapter 12, Number Sections)

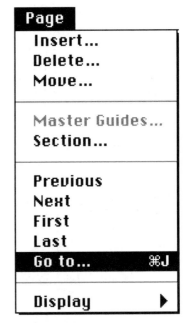

Figure 9. *Select **Previous**, **Next**, **First**, **Last**, or **Go to** from the **Page** menu.*

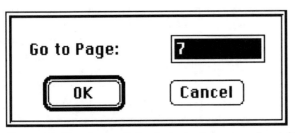

Figure 10. *The **Go to** dialog box can be accessed quickly by holding down Command (⌘) and pressing "J".*

Figure 11. *Select **Show Document Layout** from the **View** menu.*

To move through a document using the Document Layout palette:

1. Select Show Document Layout from the View menu **(Figure 11)**.

2. Double-click any page icon **(Figure 12)**.

✔ Tip

■ The page icon corresponding to the first page in a Section will be marked with an asterisk. Page icons are numbered according to the position of the corresponding pages in the document.

(See Chapter 12, Number Sections)

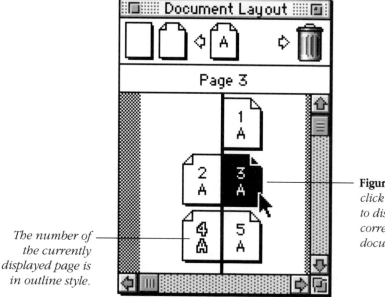

The number of the currently displayed page is in outline style.

Figure 12. *Double-click a page icon to display the corresponding document page.*

Move Through a Document

Figure 1. *The Tool palette.*

—— *The* **Text Box tool**.

In QuarkXPress, text is inputted or imported into text boxes.

To create a text box:

1. Select the Text Box tool. The cursor will temporarily turn into a crosshair icon **(Figure 1)**.

2. Press and drag in any direction. When the mouse is released the finished box will be selected and ready for input **(Figures 2a-b)**.

Figure 2a. *Press and drag with the Text Box tool.*

Figure 2b. *A new text box is created.*

To resize a text box manually:

1. Select the Item or Content tool.

2. Click on a box.

3. Press and drag any handle **(Figures 3-4)**.

✔ Tips

■ Make sure the point of the cursor arrow is directly over one of the box handles before pressing the mouse. The cursor will change into a pointing hand icon.

■ To resize a box and preserve its original proportions, hold down Option and Shift while dragging.

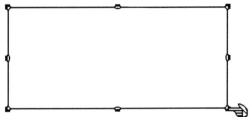

Figure 3. *Press and drag any of the four corner handles of a box.*

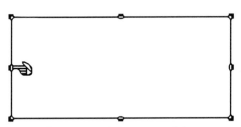

Figure 4 *Press and drag any of the four midpoint handles of a box.*

To resize a text box using the Measurements palette:

1. Select the Item or Content tool.

2. Click on a box.

3. Next to the W in the Measurements palette, enter a number in increments as small as .001 to modify the width of the box **(Figure 5)**.

   and/or

   Next to the H in the Measurements palette, enter a number to modify the height of the box.

4. Press Return.

✔ Tip

■ Numbers can be entered in any of the measurement systems used in QuarkXPress. Be sure to include the proper abbreviation, such as "p" or "mm," if the number is in a measurement system other than the default measurement system.

   (See Chapter 1, Measurement Systems)

The **horizontal position** *of the box. The number can be replaced, or a plus or minus sign and a specified amount can be entered to the right of the current number.*

The **width** *of the box.*

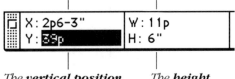

The **vertical position** *of the box.*

The **height** *of the box.*

Figure 5. *In this illustration of the Measurements palette, numbers in the fields have been entered in different measurement systems.*

Item

Modify...	⌘M
Frame...	⌘B
Runaround...	⌘T
Duplicate	⌘D
Step and Repeat...	
Delete	**⌘K**
Group	⌘G
Ungroup	⌘U
Constrain	
Lock	⌘L
Send to Back	
Bring to Front	
Space/Align...	
Picture Box Shape	▶
Reshape Polygon	

Figure 6. Select a box, then select **Delete** *from the* **Item** *menu.*

Mrs. Trenor was a tall, fair woman whose height just saved her from redundancy. Her rosy blondness had survived some forty years of futile activity without showing much trace of ill-usage except in a diminished

Figure 7a. *Make sure the cursor turns into an Item tool icon before you drag the mouse. A text box, as well as any other item, can be dragged from one page to another.*

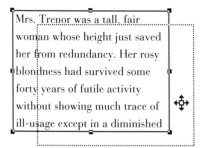

Figure 7b. *If you do not pause for the text to redraw, only the outline of the box will be displayed as it is moved.*

To delete a text box:

1. Select the **Item** or **Content** tool.
2. Click on a text box.
3. Select Delete from the Item menu **(Figure 6)**.
   or
   Hold down Command (⌘) and press "K".

✔ Tip

- A text box selected with the Item tool can also be deleted by pressing Delete on the keyboard or selecting Clear from the Edit menu.

To move a text box manually:

1. Select the Item tool.
2. Press inside a text box, pause briefly for the text to redraw, then drag **(Figures 7a-b)**.

✔ Tip

- Hold down Shift as you drag to constrain the movement to a horizontal or vertical axis. Release the mouse before releasing Shift.

To reposition a text box using the Measurements palette:

1. Select the Item or Content tool.
2. Click on a text box.
3. Enter a number next to the X in the Measurements palette to modify the horizontal position of the box relative to the ruler origin **(Figure 5)**.
   and/or
   Enter a number next to the Y in the Measurements palette to modify the vertical position of the box relative to the ruler origin.
4. Press Return.

   (See also Chapter 9, Use a Guide to Position a Box)

Delete a Text Box; Move a Text Box

To input text:

1. Create a new text box.
   (See Create a Text Box in this chapter)
   or
   Click in an already existing box to create an insertion point.
2. Select the Content tool.
3. Make sure the text box is still selected, then begin to type **(Figure 8)**.

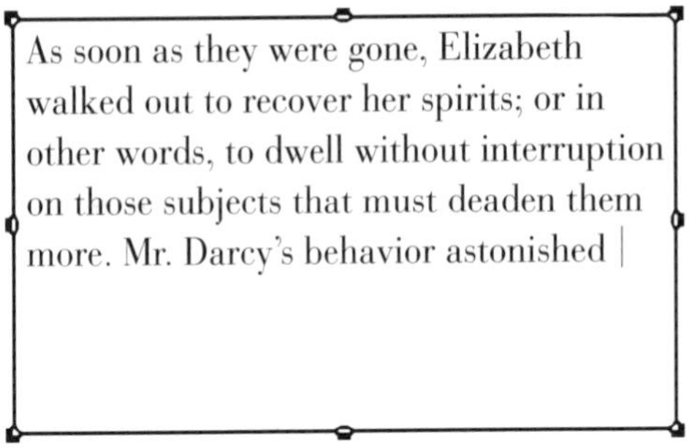

✔ Tips

- Press Return as you are typing to begin a new paragraph.
- Select Show Invisibles from the View menu to reveal paragraph returns, spaces, and other non-printing characters **(Figure 9)**.
- To position the first line of text in a box a specified distance from the top of the box, select Modify from the Item menu and enter a number in the First Baseline field.
  (See Text Inset in this chapter)

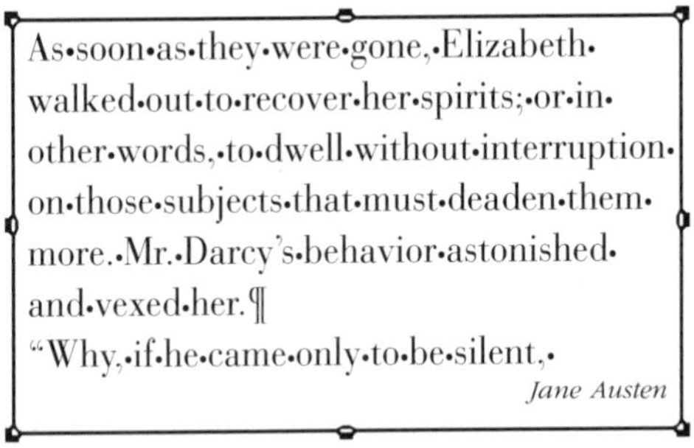

Figure 8. *Text is typed into a text box with the Content tool selected.*

Figure 9. *Press Return to begin a new paragraph. Select Show Invisibles from the View menu to display paragraph returns and other non-printing characters.*

What does the text overflow symbol mean?

If a text box is too small to display all the text that it contains, a text overflow symbol will appear in the lower right-hand corner of the box **(Figure 10)**. The text overflow symbol will disappear if the text box is enlarged enough to display all the type that it contains.

✔ Tip

- The text overflow symbol does not print. It is merely an indicator that there is text in the buffer. Only the text that is visible in the box will print.

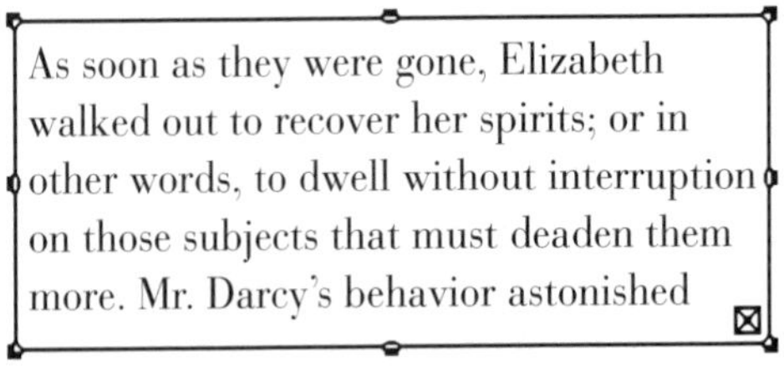

Figure 10. *The text overflow symbol appears when a box is too small to display all the text that it contains.*

On an exceptionally hot evening early in July a young man came out of the garret in which he lodged in S. Place and walked slowly, as though in hesitation, towards K. Bridge.

He had successfully avoided meeting his landlady on the ▮staircase.▮ His garret was under the roof of a high, five-storied-

Figure 11. *Double-click to highlight a **word**.*

On an exceptionally hot evening early in July a young man came out of the garret in which he lodged in S. Place and walked slowly, as though in hesitation, towards K. Bridge.

▮He had successfully avoided meeting▮ his landlady on the staircase. His garret was under the roof of a high, five-storied

Figure 12. *Triple-click to highlight a **line**.*

▮On an exceptionally hot evening early in July a young man came out of the garret in which he lodged in S. Place and walked slowly, as though in hesitation, towards K. Bridge.▮

He had successfully avoided meeting his landlady on the staircase. His garret was under the roof of a high, five-storied

Figure 13. *Click four times to highlight a **paragraph**.*

To highlight text:

1. Select the Content tool.

2. Press and drag over the text to be highlighted.

or

Click the following number of times:

1 click	To create an **insertion point**
2 clicks	To highlight a **word and the space following it**
3 clicks	To highlight a **line**
4 clicks	To highlight a **paragraph**
5 clicks	To highlight a **story**

(Figures 11-13)

✔ Tips

■ If a box is deselected and then selected again with the Content tool, the last group of characters highlighted will be highlighted again. To create a new insertion point, click once more in the text box.

■ A story can also be highlighted by selecting the Content tool, clicking in a text box, then choosing **Select All** from the Edit menu. A story consists of text contained in one box or a series of linked boxes.

■ If Select All is chosen with the **Item** tool selected, all items on the currently displayed page or spread and surrounding pasteboard will be selected.

■ Text can also be highlighted by clicking in a text box at the beginning of a desired selection, then holding down Shift and clicking at the end of the selection.

Highlight Text

To delete one character:

1. Select the Content tool.

2. Click to the right of a character to be deleted **(Figure 14)**.

3. Press Delete.

✔ Tip

■ Press the left or right pointing arrow key on the keyboard to move the insertion point one character at a time.

Figure 14. *If the Delete key were pressed with the cursor in this insertion point, the "S" would be deleted.*

To delete more than one character:

1. Select the Content tool.

2. Highlight the text that is to be deleted **(Figure 15)**.

3. Press Delete.

Figure 15. *If the Delete key were pressed with this selection highlighted, the "HES" would be deleted.*

About the Clipboard:

The **Clipboard** is a holding area that stores one cut or copied selection at a time. The current contents of the Clipboard can be retrieved an unlimited number of times with the Paste command. The Cut, Copy and Paste commands are found under the Edit menu **(Figure 16)**. The Clipboard contents are purged when you quit the application and when the computer is shut down or restarted.

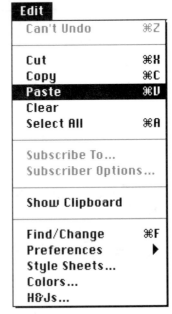

Figure 16. *The Clipboard is accessed via the **Cut, Copy** and **Paste** selections under the **Edit** menu.*

Delete Text; The Clipboard

Hip.	Well shone, moon—Truly, the moon shines with a good grace.
Dem.	Well roared, lion.
The.	Well run, Thisbe.
The.	Well moused, lion.

Figure 17a. *To move text, highlight it, then select **Cut** from the **Edit** menu.*

Dem.	Well roared, lion.
The.	Well run, Thisbe.
The.	Well moused, lion.

Figure 17b. *Click to create a new insertion point.*

Dem.	Well roared, lion.
The.	Well run, Thisbe.
Hip.	Well shone, moon—Truly, the moon shines with a good grace.
The.	Well moused, lion.
	William Shakespeare

Figure 17c. *Select **Paste** from the **Edit** menu.*

To rearrange text using the Clipboard:

1. Select the Content tool.

2. Highlight the text that is to be moved **(Figure 17a)**.

3. Select **Cut** from the Edit menu to place the highlighted text on the Clipboard and **remove** it from its current location.

or

Select **Copy** from the Edit menu to place a copy of the highlighted text on the Clipboard and **leave** the highlighted text in its current location.

4. Click in the text to create a new insertion point **(Figure 17b)**.

5. Select **Paste** from the Edit menu **(Figure 17c)**.

✔ Tips

■ The Clipboard can also be used to cut or copy a text box, picture box, line, or group with the Item tool selected, or a picture with the Content tool selected. Be sure to Paste using the same tool that was used to Cut or Copy.

■ A text box that is linked to another text box cannot be cut or copied.

(See Chapter 6, Link Text Boxes)

Accessing the Clipboard using the keyboard.	
Cut	Command + **X**
Copy	Command + **C**
Paste	Command + **V**

To frame a text box:

1. Select the Item or Content tool.

2. Click on a box.

3. Select Frame from the Item menu **(Figure 18)**.
   or
   Hold down Command (⌘) and press "B".

4. Select a preset width from the Width pop-up menu **(Figure 19)**.
   or
   Enter a custom width between .001 and 504 points in the Width field.

   Steps 5-7 are optional.

5. Select an alternate style from the Style window.

6. Select a color from the Color pop-up menu.

7. Select a shade from the Shade pop-up menu or enter a percentage in the Shade field in increments as small as .1%.

8. Click OK or press Return **(Figure 20)**.

✔ Tip

■ Enter 0 in the Width field to remove a frame.

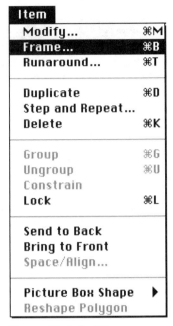

Figure 18. *Select **Frame** from the **Item** menu.*

Figure 19. *The Frame Specifications dialog box.*

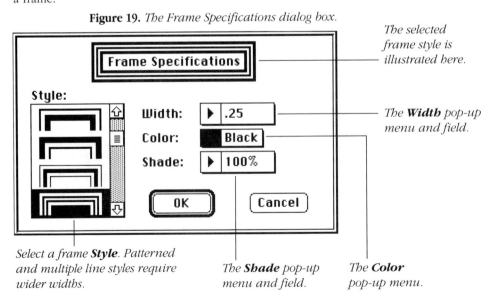

The selected frame style is illustrated here.

The **Width** pop-up menu and field.

Select a frame **Style**. Patterned and multiple line styles require wider widths.

The **Shade** pop-up menu and field.

The **Color** pop-up menu.

Figure 20. *Frames of varying styles and widths can be used to embellish boxes.*

SPEAK what you think now in hard words, and to-morrow speak what to-morrow thinks in hard words again, though it contradict every thing you said to-day.—"Ah, so you shall be sure to be misunderstood."—Is it so bad, then, to be misunderstood? Pythagoras was misunderstood, and Socrates, and Jesus, and Luther, and Copernicus, and Galileo, and Newton, and every pure and wise spirit that ever took flesh. To be great is to be misunderstood.

Ralph Waldo Emerson

Fish,

like

guests,

smell

after

three

days.

If you have built castles in the air, your work need not be lost; that is where they should be. Now put the foundations under them.

Henry David Thoreau

DO I CONTRADICT MYSELF?

VERY WELL THEN...

I CONTRADICT MYSELF;

I AM LARGE...

I CONTAIN MULTITUDES.

W a l t   W h i t m a n

Matzoh-Ball Soup

2 T. chicken fat (schmaltz)
2 large eggs, beaten
1 cup matzoh meal
Freshly ground pepper
Nutmeg
1 T. parsley, minced
1 lb. helium
4 cups chicken broth

1. Place matzoh meal in a bowl. Add 1 cup boiling water and mix well.

2. Add schmaltz, eggs, parsley, and helium and mix well. Season to taste with pepper and nutmeg.

3. Refrigerate for at least a half hour.

4. Bring chicken broth to a boil in a large saucepan.

5. Roll dough into balls about 1" in diameter.

6. Drop matzoh balls into broth one at a time, boil gently for 15 minutes, and serve.

Frame a Text Box

About Text Inset:

The Text Inset feature is used to adjust the space between text and the four edges of the box that contains it. A Text Inset value greater than zero should be applied to a box with a frame.

To modify the Text Inset:

1. Select a text box.

2. Select Modify from the Item menu **(Figure 21)**.

3. Enter an amount in the Text Inset field **(Figure 22)**.

4. Click OK or press Return **(Figures 23-24)**.

Figure 21. *Select* ***Modify*** *from the* ***Item*** *menu.*

Item	
Modify...	⌘M
Frame...	⌘B
Runaround...	⌘T
Duplicate	⌘D
Step and Repeat...	
Delete	⌘K
Group	⌘G
Ungroup	⌘U
Constrain	
Lock	⌘L
Send to Back	
Bring to Front	
Space/Align...	
Picture Box Shape	▶
Reshape Polygon	

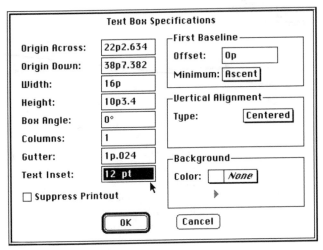

Figure 22. *The* ***Text Inset*** *field in the* ***Text Box Specifications*** *dialog box.*

PROMOTE THEN AS AN OBJECT OF PRIMARY IMPORTANCE, INSTITUTIONS FOR THE GENERAL DIFFUSION OF KNOWLEDGE. IN PROPORTION AS THE STRUCTURE OF A GOVERNMENT GIVES FORCE TO PUBLIC OPINION, IT IS ESSENTIAL THAT PUBLIC OPINION BE ENLIGHTENED.

Figure 23. *A text box with a text inset of 0 pt.*

PROMOTE THEN AS AN OBJECT OF PRIMARY IMPORTANCE, INSTITUTIONS FOR THE GENERAL DIFFUSION OF KNOWLEDGE. IN PROPORTION AS THE STRUCTURE OF A GOVERNMENT GIVES FORCE TO PUBLIC OPINION, IT IS ESSENTIAL THAT PUBLIC OPINION BE ENLIGHTENED. *George Washington*

Figure 24. *A text box with a text inset of 8 pt.*

Text Inset

Figure 25. *The rotation angle of a text box.*

X: 8p5.386	W: 12p.614	⊿ 0°
Y: 3p	H: 10p6	⟋ 0p

To rotate a text box using the Measurements palette:

1. Select the Item or Content tool.

2. Click on a text box.

3. In the rotation field on the Measurements palette, enter a positive number to rotate the box counterclockwise or a negative number to rotate the box clockwise between -360° and 360° in increments as small as .001° **(Figure 25)**.

4. Press Return.

To rotate a text box using the Rotation tool:

1. Select the Rotation tool **(Figure 26)**.

2. Click on a text box.

3. Press to create an axis point for rotation, then pause briefly for the text to redraw.

4. Drag the mouse away from the axis to create a "lever" **(Figure 27)**.

5. Drag the mouse clockwise or counterclockwise to rotate the box **(Figure 28)**.

✔ Tip

■ Hold down Shift while dragging to rotate in 45° increments.

Figure 26.
*The **Rotation tool**.*

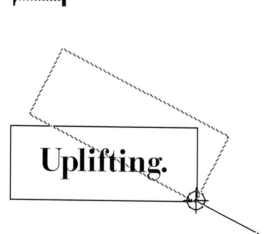

Figure 27. *If you drag away from the axis point before rotating, you will create a "lever," and the rotation will be easier to control.*

Figure 28. *A text box rotated to an angle of 90°.*

Text boxes can be made "see-through" so that they can be layered on top of each other.

To make a box transparent:

1. Select the Item or Content tool.

2. Select the text box that is to be on the top layer.

3. Select Runaround from the Item menu **(Figure 29)**.

4. Select None from the Mode pop-up menu **(Figure 30)**.

5. Click OK or press Return.

6. Select Modify from the Item menu **(Figure 29)**.

7. Select a Background Color of None. Selecting Black with a shade of 0% will not result in the same effect **(Figure 31)**.

8. Click OK or press Return.

9. With the text box still selected, select Bring to Front from the Item menu **(Figure 29)**.

10. Click in the margin or pasteboard to deselect any selected boxes and cause the screen to redraw **(Figures 32-35)**.

Figure 29.
Runaround,
Modify, *and*
Bring to Front
are all selected
from the
Item menu.

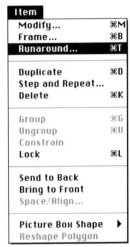

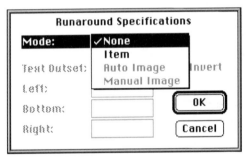

Figure 30. *Select **None** from the **Mode** pop-up menu.*

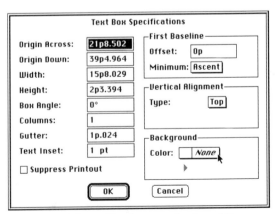

Figure 31. *Select a **Background** color of **None**.*

Layer Text Boxes

Figure 32. *A variety of effects can be created by making boxes see-through. This shadow effect was created using two text boxes. A shade of 30% was applied to the "shadow" type.*

Figure 33. *Boxes can be rotated and made transparent.*

Figure 34. *Boxes can be layered to create an illusion of depth.*

Layer Text Boxes

Figure 35. *Text boxes can be layered on top of a picture box.*

To wrap the text of one box around another box:

1. Create a new text box on top of an existing text box.
   (See Create a Text Box in this chapter)

2. With the new box still selected, select Runaround from the Item menu **(Figure 36)**.

3. Select Item from the Mode pop-up menu **(Figure 37)**.

4. Enter a number in the Top, Left, Bottom and Right fields to adjust the space between the text box and the type wrapping around it.

5. Click OK or press Return **(Figures 38-39)**.

✔ Tip

■ Text can also be wrapped around an existing box. The box that is to have text wrapped around it must be in front. Select it and choose Bring to Front from the Item menu, if necessary. *(See Chapter 15, Layer Items)*

Figure 36. *Select **Runaround** from the **Item** menu.*

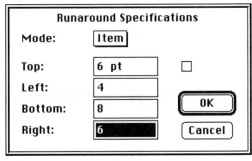

Figure 37. *Select **Item** from the **Mode** pop-up menu.*

We thus learn that man is descended from a hairy, tailed quadruped, probably arboreal in its habits, and an inhabitant of the Old World. This creature, if its whole structure had been examined by a naturalist, would have been classed amongst the Quadrumana, as surely as the still more ancient progenitor of the Old and New World monkeys.

> **We thus learn that man is descended from a hairy, tailed quadruped, probably arboreal in its habits, and an inhabitant of the Old World.**

The Quadrumana and all the higher mammals are probably derived from an ancient marsupial animal, and this through a long series of diversified forms, from some amphibian-like creature, and this again

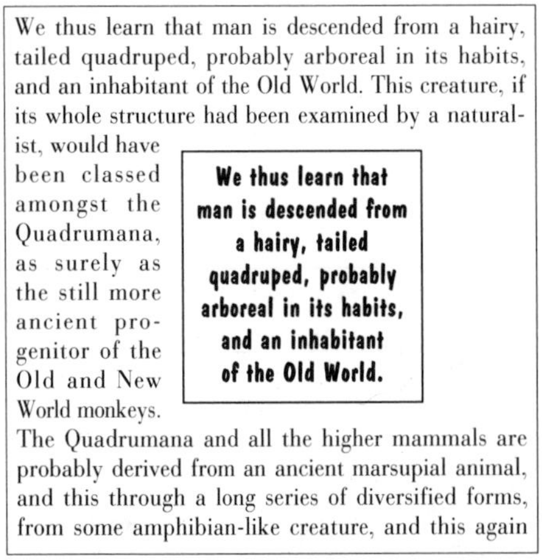

Figure 38. *Text will only wrap around **three** sides of a box that is placed **within a column**.*

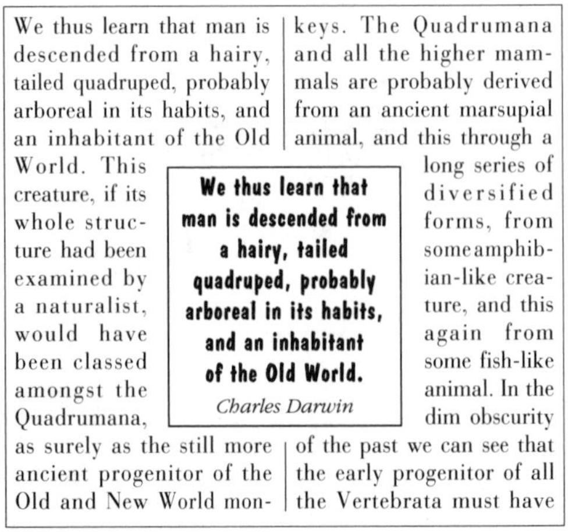

We thus learn that man is descended from a hairy, tailed quadruped, probably arboreal in its habits, and an inhabitant of the Old World. This creature, if its whole structure had been examined by a naturalist, would have been classed amongst the Quadrumana, as surely as the still more ancient progenitor of the Old and New World mon- keys. The Quadrumana and all the higher mammals are probably derived from an ancient marsupial animal, and this through a long series of diversified forms, from some amphibian-like creature, and this again from some fish-like animal. In the dim obscurity of the past we can see that the early progenitor of all the Vertebrata must have

> **We thus learn that man is descended from a hairy, tailed quadruped, probably arboreal in its habits, and an inhabitant of the Old World.**
> *Charles Darwin*

Figure 39. *Text will wrap around **all four** sides of a box if it **straddles two columns**.*

Wrap Text Around a Box

Follow these instructions to modify the number of columns and gutter width in an individual box. To change the non-printing margin and column guides or to change the number of columns in a box originating from a master page, see Chapter 12, Modify Guides and Modify a Master Page.

To modify columns using the Measurements palette:

1. Select the Item or Content tool.

2. Select a text box.

3. Enter a number in the "Cols" field on the Measurements palette **(Figure 40)**.

4. Press Return.

Figure 40. *The number of columns in a text box can be modified using the Measurements palette.*

To modify columns and/or gutter width using the Modify dialog box:

1. Select the Item or Content tool.

2. Select a text box.

3. Select Modify from the Item menu **(Figure 36)**.

4. Enter a number between 1 and 30 in the Columns field **(Figure 41)**.
and/or
Enter a number in the Gutter field.

5. Click OK or press Return.

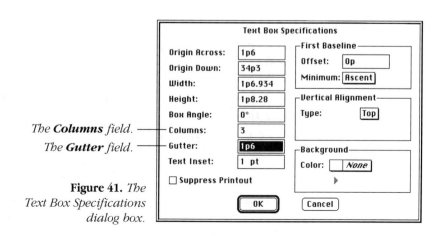

*The **Columns** field.*
*The **Gutter** field.*

Figure 41. *The Text Box Specifications dialog box.*

About Save Text:

Text in a QuarkXPress file can be saved in a word processing file format. The text in the QuarkXPress file is not affected.

To save text as a word processing file:

1. Select the Content tool.

2. Highlight text to be saved.
or
Click in a story.

3. Select Save Text from the File menu **(Figure 42)**.

4. Enter a title in the Save Text as field **(Figure 43)**.

5. If text is highlighted in the document, click Entire Story or Selected Text. If you clicked in a story, only the Entire Story option will be available.

6. Select a file format from the Format pop-up menu.

7. Select a location in which to save the text file.

8. Click Save.

✔ Tips

■ The import/export filter for the chosen word processing file format must be in the QuarkXPress folder.

■ Text saved in the ASCII format will be stripped of all formatting. Text saved in a word processing application format may be stripped of some formatting. Text saved in the XPress Tags format will retain all formatting, but will be displayed with special codes.

File

New...	⌘N
Open...	⌘O
Close	
Save	⌘S
Save as...	
Revert to Saved	
Get Text...	⌘E
Save Text...	
Save Page as EPS...	
Document Setup...	
Page Setup...	
Print...	⌘P
Quit	⌘Q

Figure 42. *Select **Save Text** from the **File** menu.*

Figure 43. *The Save Text dialog box.*

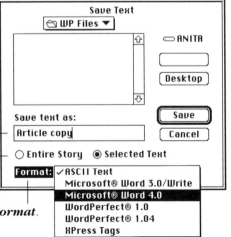

*Enter a title in the **Save Text as** field.*

*Click **Entire Story** or **Selected Text** (if available).*

*Select a file **Format.***

Save Text

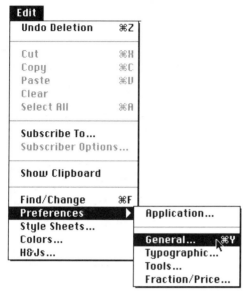

Edit

Undo Deletion	⌘Z
Cut	⌘H
Copy	⌘C
Paste	⌘U
Clear	
Select All	⌘A
Subscribe To...	
Subscriber Options...	
Show Clipboard	
Find/Change	⌘F
Preferences ▶	
Style Sheets...	
Colors...	
H&Js...	

Application...
General... ⌘Y
Typographic...
Tools...
Fraction/Price...

Figure 1. *Select **General** from the **Preferences** pop-up menu under the **Edit** menu.*

About auto page insertion:

When Auto Page Insertion and Automatic Text Box are both turned on, and text is imported *or* input into an automatic text box, new pages are added, if necessary, to contain any overflow text. Text boxes will be linked from page to page.

To turn on auto page insertion:

1. Select New from the File menu to create a new document.

2. Check the Automatic Text Box box.

3. Define the Page Size, Margin Guides, and Column Guides.
   (See Chapter 3, Create a New File)

4. Click OK or press Return.

5. Select General from the Preferences pop-up menu under the Edit menu **(Figure 1)**.

6. Select End of Story, End of Section, or End of Document from the Auto Page Insertion pop-up menu **(Figure 2)**.

7. Click OK or press Return.

Auto Page Insertion

General Preferences for IMPORTING TEXT

Horizontal Measure:	Picas	Points/Inch:	72
Vertical Measure:	Picas	Ciceros/cm:	2.1967
Auto Page Insertion:	✓Off	Snap Distance:	6
Framing:	**End of Story**	☐ Render Above:	24 pt
Guides:	End of Section	⊠ Greek Below:	5 pt
	End of Document		
Item Coordinates:	Page	☐ Greek Pictures	
Auto Picture Import:	On (verify)		
Master Page Items:	Delete Changes	⊠ Accurate Blends	
		☐ Auto Constrain	

[OK] [Cancel]

Figure 2. *Select **End of Story, End of Section** or **End of Document** from the **Auto Page Insertion** pop-up menu in the General Preferences dialog box.*

About importing text:

Text files created in word processing programs, such as Microsoft Word, can be imported into QuarkXPress. The import filter for the chosen file format must be in the QuarkXPress folder on the same level as the application when it is launched.

To import text:

1. *Optional:* Turn on Auto Page Insertion. *(See instructions on the previous page)*

2. Select the Content tool.

3. Click in a text box. Click in an automatic text box for auto page insertion. (If Auto Page Insertion is Off, the imported text will flow into a single box or a series of manually linked boxes, but new pages will not be added.) *(See Link Text Boxes in this chapter)*

4. Select Get Text from the File menu **(Figure 3)**.
or
Hold down Command (⌘) and press "E".

5. Make sure the Convert Quotes box is checked **(Figure 4)**.

6. Select a text file and click Open.
or
Double-click a text file **(Figures 5a-6b)**.

File	
New...	⌘N
Open...	⌘O
Close	
Save	⌘S
Save as...	
Revert to Saved	
Get Text...	⌘E
Save Text...	
Save Page as EPS...	
Document Setup...	
Page Setup...	
Print...	⌘P
Quit	⌘Q

Figure 3. *Select **Get Text** from the **File** menu to import a word processing file.*

Figure 4. *The Get Text dialog box.*

Select a file to be imported.

The **Type** of the selected file is indicated here.

Check the **Convert Quotes** box to convert straight quotes into curly quotes and double hyphens into em dashes.

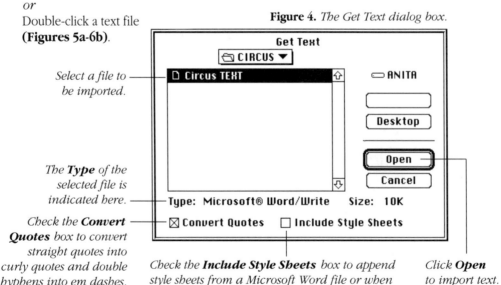

Check the **Include Style Sheets** box to append style sheets from a Microsoft Word file or when importing an ASCII file with style tag codes.

Click **Open** to import text.

Import Text

Auto Page Insertion on:

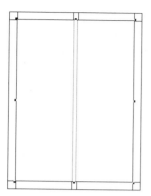

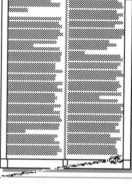

Figure 5b. *New pages are created automatically to accommodate the imported word processing file, and text is linked in a continuous flow.*

Figure 5a. *Auto Page Insertion is **on** and the automatic text box is selected. Then a word processing file is imported.*

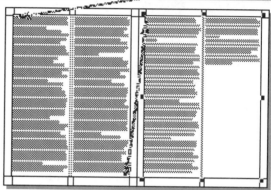

Auto Page Insertion off:

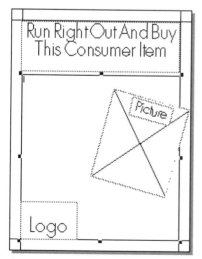

Figure 6a. *Auto Page Insertion is **off**, and a text box is selected.*

Figure 6b. *The text overflow symbol appears after the text is imported.*

Import Text

To insert blank pages using the Page menu:

Steps 1-3 are optional.

1. Select Go to from the Page menu **(Figure 7)**.

2. Enter the number of the page that is to have text inserted before or after it.

3. Click OK.

4. Select Insert from the Page menu **(Figure 7)**.

5. Enter the number of pages to be inserted in the Insert field **(Figure 8)**.

6. Click *before page, after page,* or *at end of document.*

7. Click OK or press Return.

✔ Tip

■ New pages can be based on a Master Page, Blank Single or Blank Facing Page. To link new pages to an automatic text chain, click in an automatic text box before selecting Insert Pages from the Page menu. Select a Master Page containing an automatic text box on which to base the new page(s), and check the Link to Current Text Chain box. *(See pages 51-53 in this chapter, and Chapter 12, About Master Pages)*

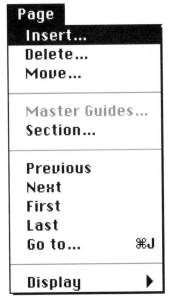

Figure 7. *The **Go to** and **Insert Pages** dialog boxes are opened from the **Page** menu.*

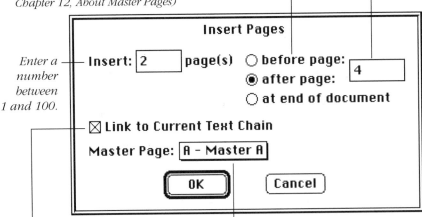

The number in this field reflects the currently displayed page. A different number can be entered.

Select a location for the inserted pages.

Enter a number between 1 and 100.

Figure 8. *The Insert Pages dialog box.*

*Check the **Link to Current Text Chain** box to link the new pages to a selected automatic text box.*

*New pages can be based on a **Master Page** or a blank page.*

Insert Pages Manually

View	
Fit in Window	⌘0
50%	
75%	
Actual Size	⌘1
200%	
Thumbnails	
Hide Guides	
Show Baseline Grid	
Snap to Guides	
Hide Rulers	⌘R
Show Invisibles	⌘I
Hide Tools	
Hide Measurements	
Show Document Layout	
Show Style Sheets	
Show Colors	
Show Trap Information	
Show Value Converter	
Windows	▶

Figure 9. *Select **Show Document Layout** from the **View** menu.*

To insert blank pages using the Document Layout palette:

1. Select Show Document Layout from the View menu **(Figure 9)**.

2. Press and drag a blank or master page icon into the document icon area **(Figure 10-14b)**.

✔ Tips

- If a page is added by dragging a blank page icon, it will have no master page applied to it. A master page can be applied to it later by dragging a master page icon over it.
  (See Chapter 12, About Master Pages and Apply a Master Page)

- Changes made using the Document Layout palette, such as adding, deleting, or rearranging pages, cannot be undone with the Undo command. Use the Revert to Saved command, if necessary.

- A page cannot be placed to the left of the first page in a facing-page document.
  (See Chapter 1, The Document Layout palette)

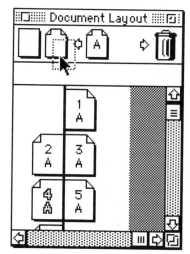

Figure 10. *Press and drag a **blank** page icon to insert a new page.*

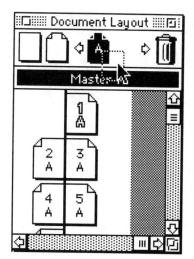

Figure 11. *Or press and drag a **master** page icon to insert a new page.*

(Continued on the following page)

Insert Pages Manually

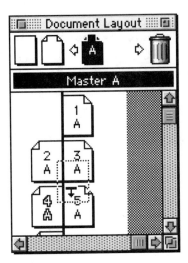

Figure 12. *To place a page between spreads in a facing-page document, release the mouse when the Force Down pointer is displayed.*

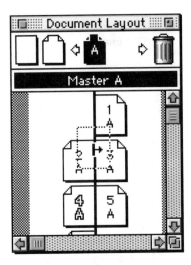

Figure 13. *In a facing-page document, releasing the mouse when the Force Right pointer is displayed may cause subsequent pages to reshuffle. Pages will not reshuffle in a single-sided document.*

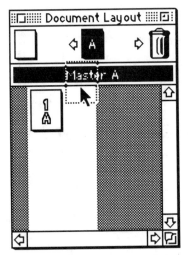

Figure 14a. *A new single-sided page can be inserted.*

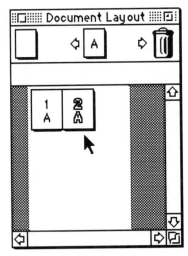

Figure 14b. *A two-page spread has been created. The two documents pages will display side-by-side on the screen. The maximum width of 48" cannot be exceeded.*

Figure 15. *Select* **Delete** *from the* **Page** *menu.*

To delete pages using the Page menu:

1. Select Delete from the Page menu **(Figure 15)**.

2. Enter a number in the first field to delete a single page.

   or

   Enter numbers in both fields to delete a series of pages **(Figure 16)**.

3. Click OK or press Return.

✔ Tip

■ If Auto Page Insertion is turned on and all the text in a linked chain does not fit on the remaining pages, new pages will be added automatically.

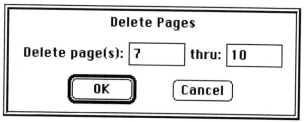

Figure 16. *Enter starting and ending page numbers to delete a series of pages.*

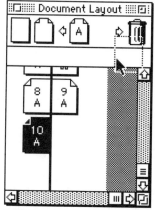

Figure 17a. *Drag a page icon or icons over the trash can icon to remove a page from a file.*

To delete pages using the Document Layout palette:

1. Select Show Document Layout from the Page menu **(Figure 9)**.

2. Press and drag a page icon over the trash can icon **(Figures 17a-b)**.

   or

   Click on the icon of the first page to be deleted, hold down Shift and click on the last page in a series of pages to be deleted, release the Shift key, then drag the group of page icons over the trash can icon.

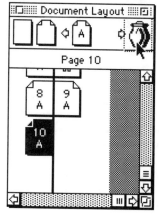

Figure 17b. *The trash can expands to indicate a page or pages are being deleted.*

3. When the prompt "Are you sure you want to remove these pages?" appears, click OK or press Return.

To rearrange pages in Thumbnails view:

1. Select Thumbnails from the View menu.

2. Select the Item or Content tool.

3. Press and drag a page icon to a new location **(Figure 18)**.

✔ Tip

■ Pages can also be **copied** from one document to another in Thumbnails view. Open two files and select Thumbnails view for both. Drag a page icon from one file into the other. A copy will be made automatically. A page cannot be copied to a document whose page size is smaller than than that of the document it is copied from. A page from a facing-page document cannot be copied to a single-sided document.

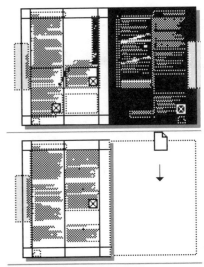

Figure 18. *Press and drag a page to a new location.*

To rearrange pages using the Document Layout palette:

1. Select Show Document Layout from the View menu **(Figure 9)**.

2. Press and drag a page icon to a new location **(Figure 19)**.

or

Click on the icon of the first page to be moved, hold down Shift and click on the icon of last page in a series of consecutive pages to be moved, release the Shift key, then drag the pages to a new location.

(See also figures on page 56)

✔ Tip

■ Pages can also be rearranged using the Move dialog box, opened from the Page menu.

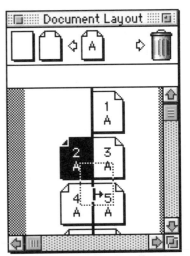

Figure 19. *When a page is forced between two pages in a facing-page document, the remaining pages may reshuffle. Note the Force Right pointer.*

Rearrange Pages

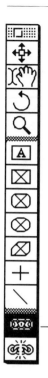

Figure 20. *Select the **Linking** tool. To keep the Linking tool selected so as to link multiple boxes, hold down Option and click on the Linking tool. A blinking marquee will appear around the tool icon in the tool palette. Deselect it by selecting another tool.*

About Linking:

Boxes can be linked so that when text is added or deleted, it will move up or down in a continuous flow from box to box. Text contained in one box or a series of linked boxes is called a story. Manual linking can be used in addition, or as an alternative, to automatic page insertion.

To link one text box to another:

1. Select the Linking tool **(Figure 20)**.

2. Click in the text box **containing** text. A blinking marquee will appear **(Figure 21)**.

3. Click on an empty text box. An arrow will appear to indicate the new link. The Linking tool will deselect automatically **(Figure 22)**.

✔ Tip

■ Linking can only occur between a box containing text and an **empty** box.

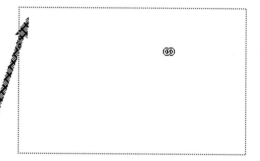

Again I see you're about to pounce,
alas, my poor computer mouse.

And losing this page I cannot afford,
but there you march across the keyboard.

You can't be hungry again so fast
Why the time's just barely passed.

Oh maybe I'll give you just a nibble,
just so you'll stay out of trib'l.

Figure 21. *Click in a box **containing text**.*

Then click in an **empty** text box.

Again I see you're about to pounce,
alas, my poor computer mouse.

And losing this page I cannot afford,
but there you march across the keyboard.

You can't be hungry again so fast
Why the time's just barely passed.

Oh maybe I'll give you just a nibble,
just so you'll stay out of trib'l.

Figure 22. *Two boxes are now linked.*

I know it's warmer than my lap,
but the printer's not the place to nap.

And I don't need your claws to catch,
the printer's pages as they hatch.

To keep you from my papers chew'n
I guess I shouldn't leave them strew'n.

I just wish you wouldn't eat'm
before I've had a chance to read'm.

Link Text Boxes

To unlink text boxes:

1. Select the Unlinking tool **(Figure 23)**.

2. Click on one of the two text boxes that are to be unlinked.

3. Click on the point or tail of the arrow between the two boxes **(Figures 24-25)**. Links preceding the break will remain intact; the link to succeeding boxes will be broken.

✔ Tip

■ If you are unable to unlink with the Unlinking tool, make sure there are no other boxes obstructing the one that you are trying to click on.

Figure 23. *Select the **Unlinking tool**.* ——

Unlink Text Boxes

Ah, what can ever be more stately and admirable to me than mast-hemm'd Manhattan?

River and sunset and scallop-edg'd waves of flood-tide?

The sea-gulls oscillating their bodies, the hay-boat in the twilight, and the belated lighter?

gods can exceed these that clasp me by the hand, and with voices I love call me promptly and loudly by my nighest name as I approach?

What is more subtle than this which ties me to the woman or man that looks in my face?

Which fuses me into you now, and pours my meaning into you?   *Walt Whitman*

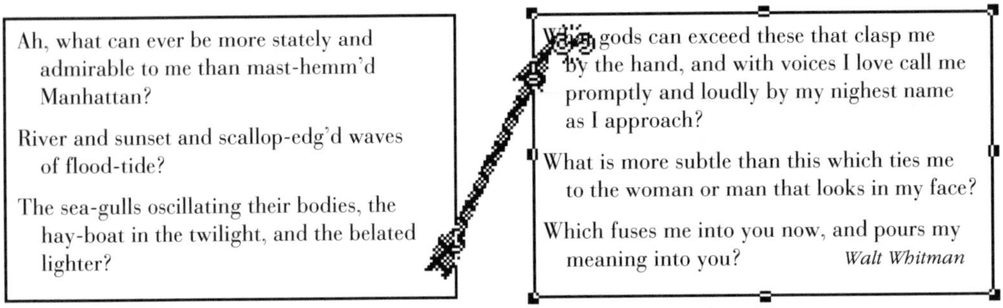

Figure 24. *Click on one of the two text boxes, and then on the point or tail of the arrow between them.*

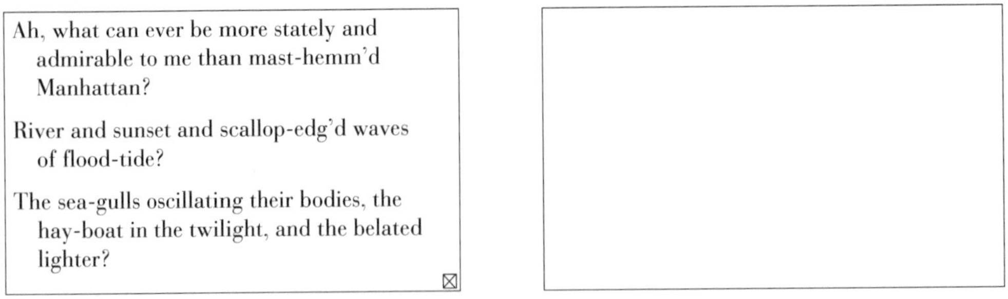

Ah, what can ever be more stately and admirable to me than mast-hemm'd Manhattan?

River and sunset and scallop-edg'd waves of flood-tide?

The sea-gulls oscillating their bodies, the hay-boat in the twilight, and the belated lighter?

Figure 25. *The link is broken.*

> **Oronte.** Do you find anything to object to in my sonnet?
>
> **Alceste.** I do not say that. But, to keep him from writing, I set before his eyes how, in our days, that desire had spoiled a great many very worthy people.

> **Oronte.** Do I write badly? Am I like them in any way?
>
> **Alceste.** I do not say that. But, in short, I said to him: What pressing need is there for you to rhyme, and what the deuce drives you into print? If we can pardon the sending into the world of a

> badly-written book, it will only be in those unfortunate men who write for their livelihood. Believe me, resist your temptations, keep these effusions from the public, and do not, how much soever you may be asked, forfeit the reputation which you enjoy at
>
> *Molière*

Figure 26. *Select the Unlinking tool, hold down **Shift** and click inside the box to be unlinked from the chain.*

To delete a box from a text chain and preserve the chain:

1. Select the Item or Content tool.

2. Select the box to be deleted.

3. Select Delete from the Item menu.

To unlink a box from a text chain and preserve the box and the chain:

1. Select the Unlinking tool **(Figure 23)**.

2. Hold down Shift and click **inside** the text box to be removed from the link chain **(Figures 26-27)**.

> **Oronte.** Do you find anything to object to in my sonnet?
>
> **Alceste.** I do not say that. But, to keep him from writing, I set before his eyes how, in our days, that desire had spoiled a great many very worthy people.

> **Oronte.** Do I write badly? Am I like them in any way?
>
> **Alceste.** I do not say that. But, in short, I said to him: What pressing need is there for you to rhyme, and what the deuce drives you into print? If we can pardon the sending into the world of a

Figure 27. *The middle box has been taken out of the chain.*

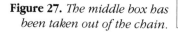

Unlink Text Boxes

About jump lines:

When text is linked between non-consecutive pages, as in a newsletter or magazine, there is usually an indicator to guide the reader to the continuation of the story or article. These "Continued On" and "Continued From" indicators are referred to as "jump lines." When the Next Box Page Number command is inserted, it is instantly converted into the page number of the next linked box in the chain. If the text is re-linked to a different page, this number is automatically updated.

Elizabeth here felt herself called on to say something in vindication of his behaviour to Wickham; and therefore gave them to understand, in as guarded a manner as she could, that by what she had heard from his relations in Kent, his actions were capable of a very different construction; and that his

Continued on page 3

Figure 28. *The text box containing the* **Next Box Page Number** *command is placed so that it overlaps the main text box.*

Figure 29. *The* **Previous Box Page Number** *command is inserted here.*

Continued from page 1

character was by no means so faulty, nor Wickham's so amiable, as they had been considered in Hertfordshire. In confirmation of this, she related the particulars of all the pecuniary transactions in which they had been connected, without actually naming her authority, but stating it to be such as might be relied on.

Jane Austen

To insert a "Continued On" command:

1. Select the Text Box tool.
2. Create a separate small box that overlaps the main text box of a story.
3. With the box still selected, choose Runaround from the Item menu and choose Item from the Mode sub-menu.
4. Click OK.
5. Select the Content tool.
6. Type any desired text into the small box, such as "Continued on page."
7. Hold down Command (⌘) and press "4" to insert the Next Box Page Number command **(Figure 28)**.

Continued from page <None>

Figure 30. *If the characters <None> appear instead of a page number, either the text box containing the Previous or Next Box Page Number command is not overlapping or inside a linked text box, or the text box it rests in is not linked to another box.*

To insert a "Continued From" command:

Follow the above instructions. For step 7, hold down Command (⌘) and press "2" to insert a Previous Box Page Number command **(Figure 29-30)**.

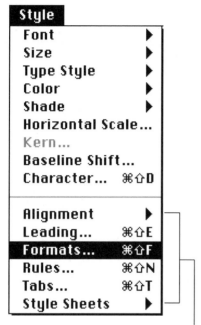

Figure 1. *The paragraph formatting features are grouped together below the dotted line under the **Style** menu.*

About paragraph formatting:

All the commands described in this chapter affect entire paragraphs rather than individual characters. These commands are grouped together under the Style menu **(Figure 1)**. A paragraph is defined as any number of characters or words followed by a Return (¶). The paragraph formatting commands can be applied to text manually or using style sheets (see Chapter 11).

To indent a paragraph:

1. Select the Content tool.

2. Click in a paragraph or press and drag through a series of paragraphs.

3. Select Formats from the Style menu **(Figure 1)**.
or
Hold down Command (⌘) and Shift and press "F".

4. Enter a number in the Left Indent and/or Right Indent fields **(Figure 2)**.

5. Click Apply to preview.

6. Click OK or press Return **(Figures 3-5)**.
(See also Figure 39a in this chapter)

Paragraph Indents

Figure 2. *Enter numbers in the **Left Indent** and/or **Right Indent** fields in the Paragraph Formats dialog box.*

Paragraph Formats

Left Indent: `4 p`	Leading: `14 pt`
First Line: `0p`	Space Before: `0p`
Right Indent: `0p`	Space After: `0p`

☐ Lock to Baseline Grid ☐ Keep with Next ¶
☐ Drop Caps ☐ Keep Lines Together

Alignment: `Left`
H&J: `Standard`

`Apply`

`OK` `Cancel`

*Click **Apply** to preview changes.*

THE MAIN CONCLUSION ARRIVED AT IN THIS WORK, NAMELY, THAT MAN IS DESCENDED FROM SOME LOWLY ORGAN- ISED FORM, WILL, I REGRET TO THINK, BE HIGHLY DISTASTEFUL TO MANY. BUT THERE CAN HARDLY BE A DOUBT THAT WE ARE DESCENDED FROM BARBARIANS.

Figure 3. *A paragraph with 0 indents.*

Paragraph Indents

THE MAIN CONCLUSION ARRIVED AT IN THIS WORK, NAMELY, THAT MAN IS DESCENDED FROM SOME LOWLY ORGANISED FORM, WILL, I REGRET TO THINK, BE HIGHLY DISTASTEFUL TO MANY. BUT THERE CAN HARDLY BE A DOUBT THAT WE ARE DESCENDED FROM BARBARIANS.

Figure 4. *A paragraph with a left indent of 2p.*

THE MAIN CONCLUSION ARRIVED AT IN THIS WORK, NAMELY, THAT MAN IS DESCENDED FROM SOME LOWLY ORGANISED FORM, WILL, I REGRET TO THINK, BE HIGHLY DISTASTEFUL TO MANY. BUT THERE CAN HARDLY BE A DOUBT THAT WE ARE DESCENDED FROM BARBARIANS.

Charles Darwin

Figure 5. *A paragraph with a right indent of 2p.*

Oronte. [To Alceste] But for you, you know our agreement. Speak to me, I pray, in all sincerity.

Alceste. These matters, sir, are always more or less delicate, and every one is fond of being praised for his wit.

But I was saying one day to a certain person, who shall be nameless, when he showed me some of his verses, that a gentleman ought at all times to exercise a great control over that itch for writing which sometimes attacks us, and should keep a tight rein over the strong propensity which one has to display such amusements; and that, in the frequent anxiety to show their productions, people are frequently exposed to act a very foolish part.

Molière

Figure 6. *A first line indent enhances readability.*

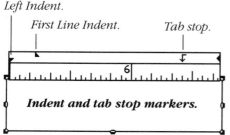

Figure 7a. *The special Paragraph Formats ruler is the width of the selected text box.*

To indent the first line of a paragraph:

1. Select the Content tool.

2. Click in a paragraph or press and drag through a series of paragraphs.

3. Select Formats from the Style menu **(Figure 1)**.
or
Hold down Command (⌘) and Shift and press "F".

4. Enter a number in the First Line field **(Figure 7b)**.

5. Click Apply to preview.

6. Click OK or press Return **(Figure 6)**.

✔ Tips

■ Indents and tab stops can be adjusted by pressing and dragging the indent and tab stop markers in the special ruler that is displayed when the Paragraph Formats dialog box is open. Insert a new tab stop by clicking in the ruler **(Figure 7a)**.
(See Set Tabs in this chapter)

■ The first paragraph after a headline or subhead is usually not indented.

■ Paragraph indent values are in addition to any Text Inset value applied to the text box.
(See Chapter 5, Text Inset)

Paragraph Indents

Figure 7b. *The **First Line** indent field in the Paragraph Formats dialog box.*

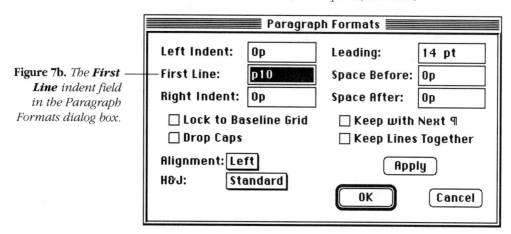

About Leading:

Leading is the distance from baseline to baseline between lines of type, and is measured in points. Three types of leading are used in QuarkXPress.

Absolute leading is an amount that remains fixed regardless of the point size of the type to which it is applied **(Figure 8)**.

Auto leading is a percentage above the point size of the largest character on each line **(Figure 9)**.

Incremental leading is equal to the type size of the largest character on each line plus or minus a specified number of points, such as +2 or -2. Both auto and incremental leading can be problematic.

To modify paragraph leading using the Measurements palette:

1. Select the Content tool.

2. Click in a paragraph or press and drag through a series of paragraphs.

3. Enter a number in the leading field in the Measurements palette **(Figure 10)**.
or
Press on the up arrow to increase the leading or the down arrow to reduce the leading in 1 point increments. Hold down Option while pressing on the arrows to increase or reduce leading in .1 point increments.

But the moment that she moved again he recognized her. The effect upon her old lover was electric, far stronger than the effect of his presence upon her. His fire, the tumultuous ring of his eloquence, seemed to go out of him. His lip struggled and trembled under the words that lay upon it; but deliver them it could not as long as she faced him. His eyes, after their first glance...

Thomas Hardy

Figure 8. *An **absolute leading** value of 11 points has been applied to this paragraph. Note that the leading is consistent regardless of the differences in point size.*

But the moment that she moved again he recognized her. The effect upon her old lover was electric, far stronger than the effect of his presence upon her. His fire, the tumultuous ring of his eloquence, seemed

Figure 9. *The same text with **auto leading**.*

Figure 10. *The leading section of the Measurements palette.*

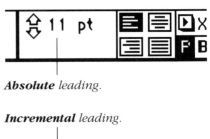

Absolute leading.

Incremental leading.

Auto leading.

Figure 11. *Select* **Leading** *from the* **Style** *menu.*

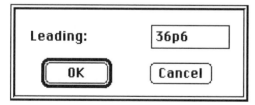

Figure 12. *The Leading dialog box.*

To modify paragraph leading using the keyboard:

1. Select the Content tool.

2. Click in a paragraph or press and drag through a series of paragraphs.

3. Hold down Command (⌘), Option and Shift and press (') to increase leading or (;) to decrease leading in 1 point increments.

To modify paragraph leading using the Leading dialog box:

1. Select the Content tool.

2. Click in a paragraph or press and drag through a series of paragraphs.

3. Select Leading from the Style menu **(Figure 11)**.

or

Hold down Command (⌘) and Shift and press "E".

4. Enter an amount an increment as small as .001 **(Figure 12)**.

5. Click OK or press Return.

✔ Tips

■ It is not necessary to enter the "pt" after the leading value.

■ Wide leading is generally used for text set in wide columns or in a sans serif font, and tight leading is used for headlines and subheads.

■ Leading values can also be modified using the Formats dialog box, opened from the Style menu.

■ Leading values do not affect the first line of text in a box. To lower text from the top of its box, select Modify from the Item menu with the box selected, and modify the Text Inset or First Baseline values in the Text Specifications dialog box.

Leading

To add space between paragraphs:

1. Select the Content tool.

2. Click in a paragraph or press and drag through a series of paragraphs.

3. Select Formats from the Style menu **(Figure 13)**.

4. Enter a number in the Space Before and/or Space After fields **(Figure 14)**.

5. Click Apply to preview.

6. Click OK or press Return **(Figure 15)**.

✔ Tip

■ The numbers entered into the Space Before and Space After fields are added together, so it is advisable to use Space After for most paragraphs, and use Space Before for special instances, such as to separate a subhead from the paragraph that precedes it.

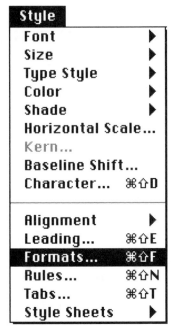

Figure 13. *Select* **Formats** *from the* **Style** *menu.*

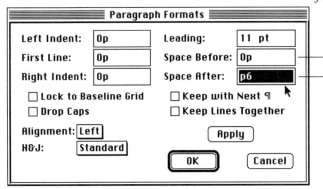

Figure 14. *The* **Space Before** *and* **Space After** *fields in the Paragraph Formats dialog box.*

O to be a Virginian where I grew up! O to be a Carolinian!
O longings irrepressible! O I will go back to old Tennessee
    and never wander more.

Mannahatta

I was asking for something specific and perfect for my city,
Whereupon lo! upsprang the aboriginal name.

Now I see what there is in a name, a word, liquid, sane, unruly,
    musical, self-sufficient,
I see that the word of my city is that word from of old,
Because I see that word nested in nests of water-bays, superb...

                                        Walt Whitman

Figure 15. *The Space Before and Space After commands offer a finer degree of control over spacing between paragraphs than does inserting extra returns.*

Add Space Between Paragraphs

About the Keep With Next ¶ command:

When this command is applied to a paragraph, the last line of the paragraph will remain attached to at least the first line of the following paragraph if it falls at the end of a column. This command can be applied to a subhead to keep it attached to the paragraph that follows it, but should not be applied to body text.

To apply the Keep With Next ¶ command:

1. Select the Content tool.

2. Click in a paragraph.

3. Select Formats from the Style menu.

4. Check the Keep With Next ¶ box **(Figure 16)**.

5. Click OK or press Return.

To apply the Keep Lines Together commands:

1. Select the Content tool.

2. Click in a paragraph.

3. Select Formats from the Style menu.

4. Check the Keep Lines Together box **(Figure 16)**.

5. Click the All Lines in ¶ button to keep all lines of a paragraph, such as a subhead, together.

or

Click the Start button to turn on "orphan and widow control." Entering "2" in both boxes ensures that no less than two lines of a paragraph are left at the top or bottom of a column.

6. Click OK or press Return.

✔ Tip

■ The Keep Lines Together command does not always work between pages.

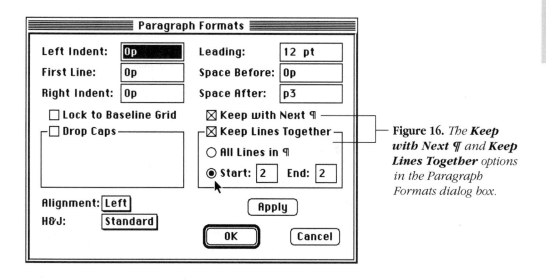

Figure 16. *The **Keep with Next ¶** and **Keep Lines Together** options in the Paragraph Formats dialog box.*

To "break" a line without creating a new paragraph:

1. Select the Content tool.

2. Click in the text where a line break is to occur.

3. Hold down Shift and press Return. With Invisibles on, a Shift-Return is displayed as a left-pointing arrow icon **(Figures 17-19)**.

✔ Tips

■ To remove a line break command, or "soft return," click at the beginning of the next line and press Delete.

■ This command can be used to adjust headlines or fix awkward breaks in ragged right copy.

Figure 17. *This is an awkward break.*

The night so luminous on the spar-deck, but otherwise on the cavernous ones below — levels so very like the tiered galleries in a coal-mine — the luminous night passed away. Like the prophet in the chariot disappearing in heaven and dropping his mantle to Elisha, the withdrawing night transferred its pale robe to the peeping day.

The night so luminous on the spar-deck, but otherwise on the cavernous ones below — levels so very like the tiered¶

galleries in a coal-mine — the luminous night passed away. Like the prophet in the chariot disappearing in heaven and dropping his mantle to Elisha, the withdrawing night transferred its pale robe to the peeping day.

Figure 18. *A paragraph return creates a new paragraph.*

The night so luminous on the spar-deck, but otherwise on the cavernous ones below — levels so very like the tiered ↵ galleries in a coal-mine — the luminous night passed away. Like the prophet in the chariot disappearing in heaven and dropping his mantle to Elisha, the withdrawing night transferred its pale robe to the peeping day.

Herman Melville

Figure 19. *A **Shift-Return** creates a new line within a paragraph.*

A quick way to copy paragraph formats from one paragraph to another within a story.

Click in a paragraph or press and drag through a series of paragraphs that are to be modified. Hold down Option and Shift and click in the paragraph whose formats you would like to copy.

Figure 20. *Select* **Formats** *from the* **Style** *menu.*

About hanging indents:

A format in which the first line of a paragraph is aligned flush left and the remaining lines are indented is referred to as a hanging indent. Hanging indents can be used to make subheads, bullets, or other special text prominent **(Figure 22)**.

To create a hanging indent using the Formats dialog box:

1. Select the Content tool.

2. Click in a paragraph or press and drag through a series of paragraphs.

3. Select Formats from the Style menu **(Figure 20)**.

4. Enter a number in the Left Indent field **(Figure 21)**.

5. Enter the same number in the First Line field preceded by a minus (-) sign.

6. Click OK or press Return.

A positive number is entered in the **Left Indent** *field.*

A negative number is entered in the **First Line Indent** *field.*

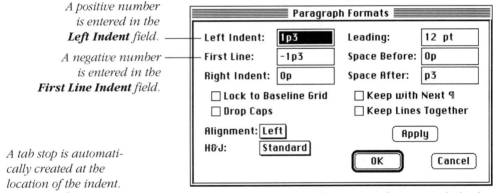

Figure 21. *The Paragraph Formats dialog box.*

A tab stop is automatically created at the location of the indent.

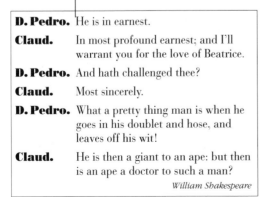

Figure 22. *Hanging indents.*

Hanging Indents

About the
Indent Here character:

The Indent Here character is used to create hanging indents. It is useful for formatting small amounts of text. However, it can be applied to only one paragraph at a time, and cannot be incorporated into a style sheet. To format more than one paragraph at a time, create hanging indents using positive and negative indents in the Formats dialog box.
(See instructions on the previous page)

THESEUS. |Now, fair Hippolyta, our nuptial hour draws on apace; four happy days bring in another moon: but, oh, methinks, how slow this old moon wanes! She lingers my desires, like to a step-dame or a dowager, long withering out a young man's revenue.

Figure 23. *To insert the Indent Here command, click in the text, hold down Command (⌘) and press "\" .*

To create a hanging
indent using the
Indent Here character:

1. Select the Content tool.

2. Click in a paragraph where the indent is to be inserted **(Figures 23-24)**.

3. Hold down Command (⌘) and press backslash (\).

THESEUS. Now, fair Hippolyta, our nuptial hour draws on apace; four happy days bring in another moon: but, oh, methinks, how slow this old moon wanes! She lingers my desires, like to a step-dame or a dowager, long withering out a young man's revenue.

Figure 24. *A hanging indent is created.*

To remove an
Indent Here character:

1. Select the Content tool.

2. Click just to the right of the Indent Here character **(Figure 25)**.

3. Press Delete.

Figure 25. *The Indent Here character displays as a vertical dotted line when Show Invisibles is selected from the View menu. Select a large view size to see it.*

THESEUS. Now, fair Hippol
hour draws on
days bring in
oh, methinks,

Figure 26. *Select* ***Formats*** *from the* ***Style*** *menu.*

To insert an automatic drop cap:

1. Select the Content tool.

2. Click in a paragraph.

3. Select Formats from the Style menu **(Figure 26)**.

4. Check the "Drop Caps" box **(Figure 27)**.

Steps 5-7 are optional.

5. Enter a number in the Character Count field to modify the number of characters to be enlarged to form the drop cap.

6. Enter a number in the Line Count field to modify the height of the drop cap. The drop cap adjusts to fit the line count; the maximum line count is 8.

7. Click Apply to preview.

8. Click OK or press Return **(Figures 28-29)**.

Figure 27. *Check the* ***Drop Caps*** *box in the Paragraph Formats dialog box.*

The number of characters to be "dropped."

The number of lines of text the drop cap will fit into.

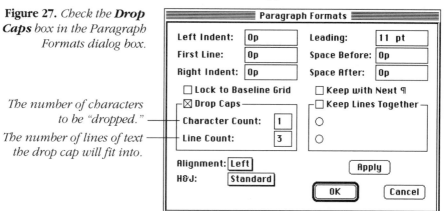

Automatic Drop Caps

Not only was her first-floor flat invaded at all hours by throngs of singular and often undesirable characters but her remarkable lodger showed an eccentricity and irregularity in his life which must have sorely tried her patience. His incredible untidiness, his addiction to music at strange hours, his occasional revolver practice within doors, his weird and often malodorous scientific experiments, and the atmosphere of violence and danger which hung around him made him the very worst tenant in London. On the other hand, his payments were princely...

Figure 28. *A drop cap with a character count of 1 and a line count of 5.*

NOT only was her first-floor flat invaded at all hours by throngs of singular and often undesirable characters but her remarkable lodger showed an eccentricity and irregularity in his life which must have sorely tried her patience. His incredible untidiness, his addiction to music at strange hours, his occasional revolver practice within doors, his weird and often malodorous scientific experiments, and the atmosphere of violence and danger which hung around him made him the very worst tenant in London. On the other hand, his payments were princely...

Figure 29. *A drop cap with a character count of 3 and a line count of 2.*

To resize an automatic drop cap manually:

1. Select the Content tool.

2. Press and drag to highlight a drop cap character or characters **(Figure 30)**.

3. In the point size field of the Measurements palette, enter a number greater than 100% to enlarge the drop cap, or a number less than 100% to reduce the drop cap. The minimum is 10% and the maximum is 400% **(Figure 31)**.

4. Press Return **(Figure 32)**.

To kern next to a drop cap:

1. Select the Content tool.

2. Click in the first line of the paragraph between the drop cap and the character to the right of it. A long blinking I-beam will appear when the cursor has been inserted correctly **(Figure 33)**.

3. In the Tracking & Kerning section of the Measurements palette, click the left arrow to delete space or the right arrow to add space **(Figure 34)**.

✔ Tip

■ Hold down Option while clicking on the left or right arrow to kern in finer increments.

To remove an automatic drop cap:

1. Select the Content tool.

2. Click in a paragraph containing a drop cap.

3. Select Formats from the Style menu.

4. Uncheck the "Drop Caps" box.

5. Click OK or press Return.

An anomaly which often struck me in the character of my friend Sherlock Holmes was that, although in his methods of thought he was the neatest and most methodical of mankind, and although also he affected a certain quiet primness of dress, he was none the less in his personal habits one of the most intidy

Figure 30. *Highlight a drop cap.*

Figure 31. *Modify the size percentage in the Measurements palette.*

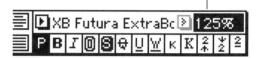

An anomaly which often struck me in the character of my friend Sherlock Holmes was that, although in his methods of thought he was the neatest and most methodical of mankind, and although also he affected a certain quiet primness of dress, he was none the less in his per-

Figure 32. *A drop cap enlarged to 125%.*

FOR THOSE WHO LIKE THIS SORT OF THING, THIS IS THE SORT OF THING THEY LIKE.

Figure 33. *The cursor positioned for kerning next to a drop cap.*

Figure 34. *The Tracking & Kerning section of the Measurements palette.*

Automatic Drop Caps

Invisible characters and the keystrokes used to produce them.

Tab	→	Tab
Word Space	.	Space bar
New Paragraph	¶	Return
New Line	↵	Shift-Return
New Column	↓	Enter
New Box	↯	Shift-Enter
Indent Here	┊	Command \

About Tabs:

Tabs are commands that are used to align columns of text or figures. Using spaces to create columns will result in uneven spacing due to variable character widths. If no custom tabs have been set, text will jump to the nearest default tab stop. Default tab stops are ½ inch apart. One set of custom tab stops can be applied per paragraph **(Figures 35-36)**.

To insert tabs into text:

1. Select the Content tool.

2. Press Tab as you input copy before typing each new column. The cursor will jump to the next tab stop.

or

To add a tab to already inputted text, click to the left of the text that is to start each new column and press Tab.

or

Hold down Option and press Tab to set a Right Indent Tab flush with the right indent of the box.

Endangered vs. non-Endangered Bears			
	1930	*1992*	*2000* (Projected)
Pandas	1 million	4 thousand	0
Koalas	6 million	3 thousand	7
Poohs	1 million	2 billion	3 billion

Figure 35. *Tabs are used to align columns of text.*

Endangered vs. non-Endangered Bears¶			
→	*1930* →	*1992* →	*2000* (Projected)

Figure 36. *Tab symbols are displayed when Show Invisibles is selected from the View menu.*

To set a custom tab stop:

1. Select the Content tool.

2. Highlight **all** the copy for which the tab stop is to be set.

3. Select Tabs from the Style menu **(Figure 37)**.
or
Hold down Command (⌘) and Shift and press "T".

4. Select Left, Center, Right, Decimal, or Comma from the Alignment pop-up menu **(Figure 38)**.

5. *Optional:* To create a leader, enter any keyboard character in the Fill Character field. Enter a period (.) to create a dot leader **(Figure 39b)**.

6. Click in the tabs ruler where the tab stop is to occur **(Figure 39a)**.
or
Enter a position number in the Position field using any measurement system, then click Apply. Click Apply after each position number is entered **(Figure 39b)**.

7. Click OK or press Return **(Figures 41-42)**.

✔ Tips

■ To move a tab stop, press and drag the tab stop marker to the left or right.

(See also the first Tip on page 65)

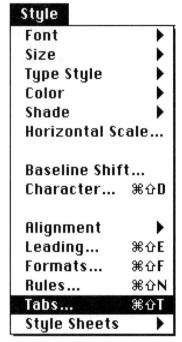

Figure 37. *Select **Tabs** from the **Style** menu.*

Figure 38. *The Paragraph Tabs dialog box.*

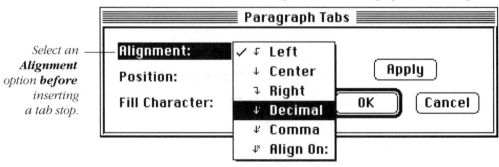

*Select an **Alignment** option **before** inserting a tab stop.*

The paragraph indent markers on the Tabs ruler can be moved to modify paragraph indents.

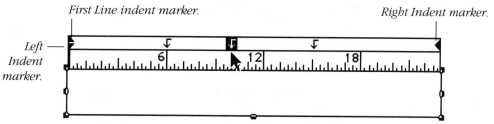

Figure 39a. *Click in the tabs ruler to insert a custom tab stop, or enter a number in the **Position** field in the Paragraph Tabs dialog box (below). A maximum of 20 tab stops can be inserted per paragraph.*

Figure 39b. *The Paragraph Tabs dialog box.*

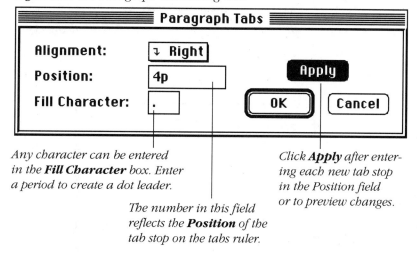

*Any character can be entered in the **Fill Character** box. Enter a period to create a dot leader.*

*Click **Apply** after entering each new tab stop in the Position field or to preview changes.*

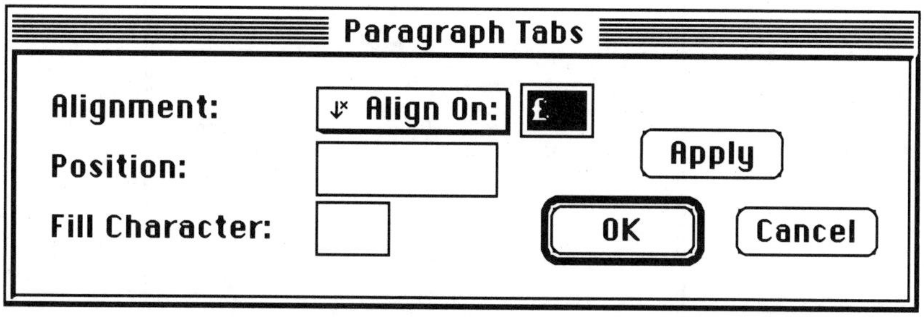

*The number in this field reflects the **Position** of the tab stop on the tabs ruler.*

Figure 40. *To align tab stops on a custom character, select **Align On** from the Alignment pop-up menu and then enter a character in the **Align On** field.*

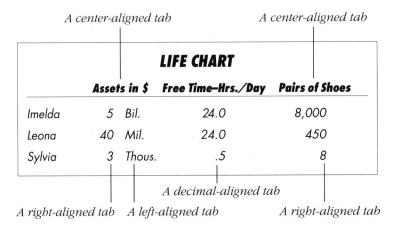

Figure 41. *Center, Left, Right and Decimal-aligned tabs were used to create this chart.*

A center-aligned tab

A center-aligned tab

LIFE CHART

	Assets in $	Free Time–Hrs./Day	Pairs of Shoes
Imelda	5 Bil.	24.0	8,000
Leona	40 Mil.	24.0	450
Sylvia	3 Thous.	.5	8

A decimal-aligned tab

A right-aligned tab   *A left-aligned tab*   *A right-aligned tab*

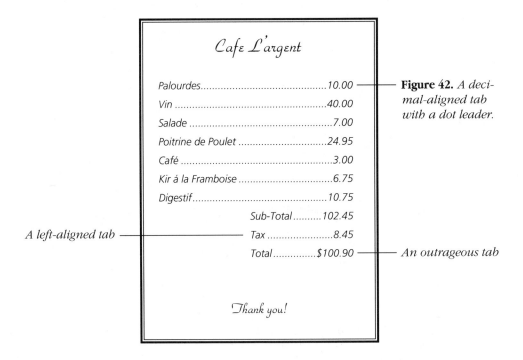

Café L'argent

Palourdes	10.00
Vin	40.00
Salade	7.00
Poitrine de Poulet	24.95
Café	3.00
Kir á la Framboise	6.75
Digestif	10.75
Sub-Total	102.45
Tax	8.45
Total	$100.90

Thank you!

Figure 42. *A decimal-aligned tab with a dot leader.*

A left-aligned tab

An outrageous tab

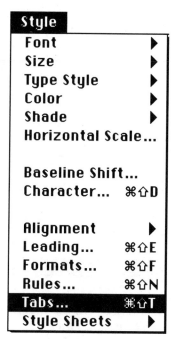

Figure 43. *Select* **Tabs** *from the* **Style** *menu.*

To remove custom tab stops:

1. Select the Content tool.

2. Highlight the text from which the tab stops are to be removed.

3. Select Tabs from the Style menu **(Figure 43)**.

4. Hold down Option and click once on the tabs ruler to remove **all** the tab stops.

or

Press and drag a tab stop marker up or down out of the ruler **(Figure 44)**.

5. Click OK or press Return.

✔ Tip

■ If two or more paragraphs are highlighted and the highlighted text contains more than one set of tab stops, only the tab stops for the first paragraph are displayed, but new tab settings will affect all highlighted text.

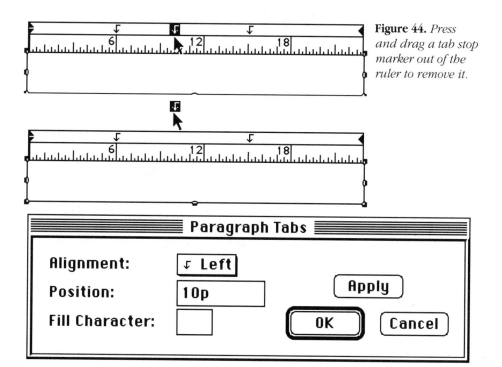

Figure 44. *Press and drag a tab stop marker out of the ruler to remove it.*

About paragraph rules:

A rule inserted using the Paragraph Rules feature remains anchored to the paragraph even if the paragraph is moved, which is not the case for lines created with the Line tools. And paragraph rules can be modified in their appearance and position, unlike the Underline style.

To insert a paragraph rule:

1. Select the Content tool.

2. Click in a paragraph or press and drag through a series of paragraphs.

3. Select Rules from the Style menu **(Figure 45)**.

or

Hold down Command (⌘) and Shift and press "N."

4. Check the Rule Above or Rule Below box. The dialog box will expand **(Figure 46)**.

5. Select a width from the Width pop-up menu or enter a custom width in the Width field **(Figure 47)**.

6. Select Indents or Text from the Length pop-up menu.

7. Highlight the entire Offset field, and enter a number in any measurement system to Offset a Rule Above from the baseline of the first line of the paragraph or Offset a Rule Below from the baseline of the last line of the paragraph.

Steps 8-11 are optional.

8. Modify the number in the From Left or From Right fields to indent the rule.

9. Select a style from the Style pop-up menu.

10. Select a color from the Color pop-up menu.

(Continued on the following page)

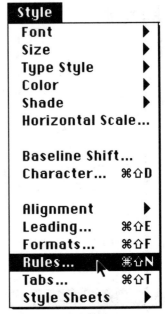

Figure 45. *Select **Rules** from the **Style** menu.*

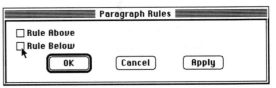

Figure 46. *The Paragraph Rules dialog box expands when the **Rule Above** or **Rule Below** box is checked (see Figure 47).*

Paragraph Rules

11. Select a shade from the Shade pop-up menu or enter a custom shade in the Shade field.

12. Click Apply to preview.

13. Click OK or press Return **(Figures 48-51)**.

✔ Tips

■ Be sure to enter an Offset for a Rule Above that is at least as large as the point size of the type. The Offset for both a Rule Above and Rule Below originates from the baseline.

■ Setting an absolute number for the Offset is preferable to using a percentage.

(Continued on the following page)

Figure 47. *The Paragraph Rules dialog box.*

*The amount a rule is indented is determined by the number in the **From Left** and/or **From Right** fields as well as any existing paragraph indents and text inset values.*

*Select **Indents** or **Text** from the Length pop-up menu.*

*Select from eleven **Styles**.*

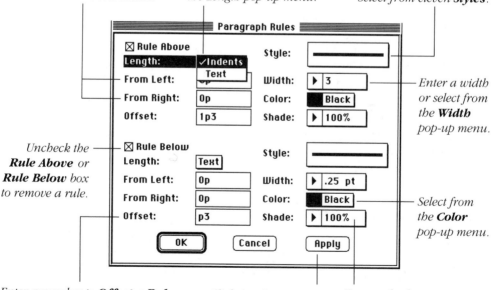

*Uncheck the **Rule Above** or **Rule Below** box to remove a rule.*

*Enter a width or select from the **Width** pop-up menu.*

*Select from the **Color** pop-up menu.*

*Enter a number to **Offset** a **Rule Above** from the baseline of the first line of the paragraph or **Offset** a **Rule Below** from the baseline of the last line of the paragraph.*

*Click **Apply** to preview.*

*Enter a shade percentage or select from the **Shade** pop-up menu.*

Paragraph Rules

Figure 48. *A "reverse" rule effect can be created by coloring text white, selecting a wide width for the rule, and using a negative Offset. A negative value of up to half the width of the rule can be entered. This is a 16 point black Rule Above, with the Indents option selected from the Length pop-up menu, Left and Right Indents of 0, and an Offset of -p4.*

E T H A N   F R O M E
By Edith Wharton

I had the story, bit by bit, from various people, and, as generally happens in such cases, each time it was a different story.

If you know Starkfield, Massachusetts, you know the post-office. If you know the post-office you must have seen Ethan Frome drive up to it, drop the reins on his hollow-backed bay and

Paragraph Rules

Rules can be used to jazz up subheads.

Rules can be used to jazz up subheads.

Figure 49. *In this example, rules of varying lengths and weights have been combined.*

Norton Thorpe clapped the young Frenchman on the shoulder and, with a hearty smile, shook his hand. "My dear chap! How could I possibly object to my daughter becoming not only the new Countess d'Auvergne but also the wife of an up-and-coming electronics genius!" Lisa, her

"How could I possibly object to my daughter becoming not only the new Countess d'Auvergne but also the wife of an up-and-coming electronics genius..."

eyes moist with tears of joy, not only because of her future marriage but also because of her restored relationship with her father, threw her arms around Nancy in a warm embrace exclaiming: "Oh, Nancy, none of this could ever have happened if you hadn't worked so hard to solve

Figure 50. *Paragraph rules can be used to separate a pull quote from body text.*

ALL

THE

REALLY GOOD

IDEAS

I EVER HAD

CAME

TO ME

WHILE I WAS

MILKING

A COW.

Grant Wood

Figure 51. *Rules can be used to emphasize headlines. In this example, a Return was inserted after every line, making every line a separate paragraph.*

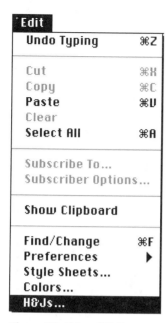

Figure 52. *Select **H&Js** from the **Edit** menu.*

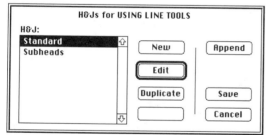

Figure 53. *Click **New** or select an H&J and click **Edit**.*

Figure 54. *The Edit Hyphenation & Justification dialog box.*

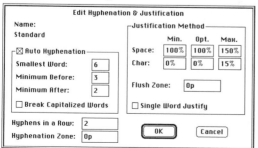

About hyphenation:

Hyphenation lessens gaps between words in justified type and smooths ragged edges in non-justified type.

Hyphenation (and Justification) specifications are stored in H&Js. A document can have several H&Js, and they are applied to paragraphs using the Paragraphs Formats dialog box.

To turn on hyphenation:

1. Select H&Js from the Edit menu **(Figure 52)**.

2. Click New to create a new H&J **(Figure 53)**.
   or
   Select an H&J and click Edit. The Standard H&J can be modified.

3. Enter a name if the H&J is new.

4. Check the Auto Hyphenation box **(Figure 54)**.

Steps 5-10 are optional.

5. In the Smallest Word field, modify the minimum number of characters a word must contain to be hyphenated.

6. In the Minimum Before field, modify the minimum number (1-6) of a word's characters that must precede a hyphen.

7. In the Minimum After field, modify the minimum number (2-8) of a word's characters to follow a hyphen.

8. Check or uncheck the Break Capitalized Words box.

9. Modify the number of consecutive lines that can end with a hyphen in the Hyphens in a Row field.

10. Enter a number larger than zero in the Hyphenation Zone field to create a more ragged edge (less hyphenation).

11. Click OK or press Return.

12. Click Save **(Figure 53)**.

   (See Apply an H&J on the following page)

To apply an H&J:

1. Select the Content tool.

2. Click in a paragraph or press and drag through a series of paragraphs.

3. Select Formats from the Style menu **(Figure 55)**.

   or

   Hold down Command (⌘) and Shift and press "F".

4. Select an H&J from the H&Js pop-up menu **(Figure 57)**.

5. Click OK or Press Return.

✔ Tips

■ The Normal style sheet will have the Standard H&J associated with it unless a different H&J is selected for it. *(See Chapter 11, Edit a Style Sheet)*

■ The new Enhanced Hyphenation Method creates better word breaks when Auto Hyphenation is turned on. Select Enhanced Hyphenation from the Hyphenation Method pop-up menu in the Typographic Preferences dialog box, opened from the Edit menu. Select Standard to use the method built into earlier versions of QuarkXPress **(Figure 56)**.

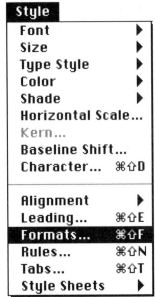

Figure 55. *Select* **Formats** *from the* **Style** *menu.*

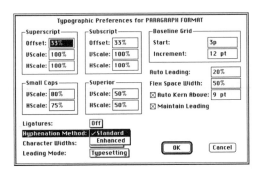

Figure 56. *Select Enhanced or Standard Hyphenation Method in the Typographic Preferences dialog box.*

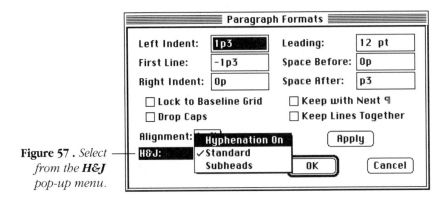

Figure 57 . *Select from the* **H&J** *pop-up menu.*

Apply an H&J

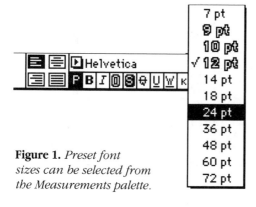

Figure 1. *Preset font sizes can be selected from the Measurements palette.*

To resize type using the Measurements palette:

1. Select the Content tool.

2. Highlight the text to be resized.

3. Select a preset size from the Size pop-up menu on the right side of the Measurements palette **(Figure 1)**.
or
In the Size field on the Measurements palette, enter a number between 2 and 720 in increments as small as .001 point. It is not necessary to enter "pt" following the number **(Figure 2)**.

4. Press Return.

✔ Tip

■ Preset point sizes can be selected from the Size pop-up menu under the Style menu, and custom point sizes can be entered in the "Other" dialog box selected from the Size pop-up menu.

Figure 2. *Point sizes between 2 to 720 can be entered in the **Size** field on the Measurements palette.*

*The **Size** pop-up menu.*

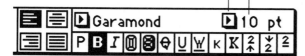

Resize Type

To resize type using the keyboard:

1. Select the Content tool.

2. Highlight the text to be resized.

3. Hold down Command (⌘) and Shift and press the < key or the > key to reduce or enlarge the text to preset sizes.
or
Hold down Command (⌘), Option, Shift and press the < key or the > key to reduce or enlarge the text in 1 point increments.

To change a font:

1. Select the Content tool.

2. Highlight the text to be modified.

3. Select a font from the Font pop-up menu in the Measurements palette **(Figure 3)**.

or

Click in the font field to the left of the current font name, type the new font name, then press Return. Entering the first few characters of the font name is usually sufficient **(Figure 4)**.

✔ Tips

■ Hold down Command (⌘), Option, Shift and press "M" to highlight the Font field on the Measurements palette.

■ Fonts can also be selected from the Font pop-up menu under the Style menu.

■ Font, Size, Color, Shade, Style, Horizontal Scale, Track Amount, and Baseline Shift modifications can be made using the Character dialog box, opened from the Style menu.

Figure 3. *Fonts are grouped by families in this Font pop-up menu with a utility called Adobe Type Reunion.*

Press this arrowhead to open the Font pop-up menu.

Or click just to the left of the current font name and type a new font name.

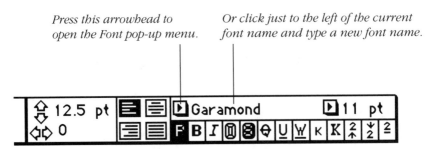

Figure 4. *The Font field on the Measurements palette.*

To style type:

1. Select the Content tool.

2. Highlight the text to be styled.

3. Click one or more of the style icons on the Measurements palette **(Figure 6)**.

✔ Tips

■ Click the "P" on the Measurements palette to remove **all** styling from highlighted type.

■ To remove **one** style at a time, click any highlighted style icon on the Measurements palette.

■ It is not advisable to input text with the Caps key locked. Lowercase characters can easily be converted into caps or small caps, but characters input with the Caps key locked cannot be converted to lowercase.

■ When the small caps style is applied to type, uppercase characters remain uppercase and lowercase characters are converted to small caps **(Figure 5)**.

■ Superscript type sits above the baseline; subscript type rests below the baseline; superior type is aligned with the cap height of the font and reduced in point size.

To style type using the keyboard.

Hold down **Command** and **Shift** and press any of the following keys:

Plain	**P**
Bold	**B**
Italic	**I**
Underline	**U**
Word Underline	**W**
Strike Thru	**/**
Outline	**O**
Shadow	**S**
All Caps	**K**
Small Caps	**H**
Superscript	**+**
Subscript	**-**
Superior	**V**

Figure 5.
Lowercase —
characters.

Small caps. —

All caps. —

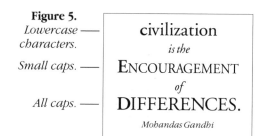

civilization
is the
ENCOURAGEMENT
of
DIFFERENCES.
Mohandas Gandhi

Style Type

Figure 6. *The style icons on the Measurements palette.*

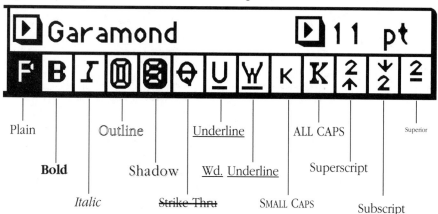

Plain   Outline   Underline   ALL CAPS   Superior

Bold   Shadow   Wd. Underline   Superscript

Italic   ~~Strike Thru~~   SMALL CAPS   Subscript

To modify horizontal alignment:

1. Select the Content tool.

2. Click in a paragraph or press and drag through a series of paragraphs.

3. Click one of the four Horizontal Alignment icons on the Measurements palette **(Figure 7-8)**.

✔ **Tips**

■ Only one alignment option can be applied per paragraph.

■ The horizontal alignment options can also be applied using the Alignment pop-up menu under the Style menu, or using the Formats dialog box, opened from the Style menu.

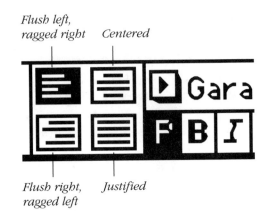

Flush left, ragged right   *Centered*

Flush right, ragged left   *Justified*

Figure 7. *The four alignment icons on the Measurements palette.*

To change the horizontal alignment of type using the keyboard.

Hold down **Command** and **Shift**, and press any of the following keys:

Flush left, ragged right	**L**
Centered	**C**
Flush right, ragged left	**R**
Justified	**J**

Flush left, ragged right —

So we was all right now, as to the shirt and the sheet and the spoon and the candles, by the help of the calf and rats and the mixed-up counting; and as to the candlestick, it warn't no consequence, it would blow over by and by....

— *Centered*

So we was all right now, as to the shirt and the sheet and the spoon and the candles, by the help of the calf and rats and the mixed-up counting; and as to the candlestick, it warn't no consequence, it would blow over by and by....

Flush right, ragged left —

So we was all right now, as to the shirt and the sheet and the spoon and the candles, by the help of the calf and rats and the mixed-up counting; and as to the candlestick, it warn't no consequence, it would blow over by and by....

— *Justified*

So we was all right now, as to the shirt and the sheet and the spoon and the candles, by the help of the calf and rats and the mixed-up counting; and as to the candlestick, it warn't no consequence, it would blow over by and by....

Mark Twain

Figure 8. *The four horizontal alignment options.*

Item	
Modify...	⌘M
Frame...	⌘B
Runaround...	⌘T
Duplicate	⌘D
Step and Repeat...	
Delete	⌘K
Group	⌘G
Ungroup	⌘U
Constrain	
Lock	⌘L
Send to Back	
Bring to Front	
Space/Align...	
Picture Box Shape	▶
Reshape Polygon	

Figure 9. *Select Modify from the Item menu.*

To modify vertical alignment:

1. Select the Item or Content tool.
2. Click on a text box.
3. Select Modify from the Item menu **(Figure 9)**.
4. Select one of the four Vertical Alignment options from the Type pop-up menu **(Figure 11)**.
5. Click OK or press Return **(Figure 10)**.

✔ Tips

■ In vertically justified text with an Inter ¶ Max value of 0, space is added evenly between lines and paragraphs. An Inter ¶ Max value greater than 0 represents the maximum space added between paragraphs before leading is affected.

■ Make sure there is no return at the end of the last line in a box with bottom, centered, or justified Vertical Alignment.

Figure 10.

Top Alignment.

Bottom Alignment.

Centered Alignment.

Justified Alignment.

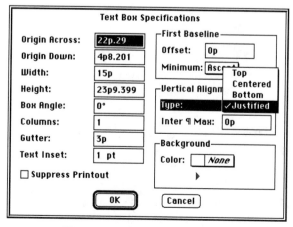

Figure 11. *The Vertical Alignment options.*

Never put off till tomorrow what you can do the day after tomorrow.

Mark Twain

Text Box Specifications

Origin Across: 22p.29
Origin Down: 4p8.201
Width: 15p
Height: 23p9.399
Box Angle: 0°
Columns: 1
Gutter: 3p
Text Inset: 1 pt
☐ Suppress Printout

First Baseline
Offset: 0p
Minimum: Asc

Vertical Align
Type:
Inter ¶ Max: 0p

Top
Centered
Bottom
✓Justified

Background
Color: None

OK   Cancel

Vertical Alignment

About tracking and kerning:

Kerning is the adjustment of space between a pair of characters when the cursor is inserted between them. **Tracking** is the adjustment of the space to the right of one or more highlighted characters. The same section of the Measurements palette is used for Tracking and Kerning.

To kern type using the Measurements palette:

1. Select the Content tool.

2. Click between two characters **(Figure 12)**.

3. Click the right arrow to add space or the left arrow to delete space **(Figure 13-14)**.

or

Enter a number between -500% and 500% in increments as small as .01 in the Tracking & Kerning field, then press Return.

To track type using the Measurements palette:

1. Select the Content tool.

2. Highlight any number of characters.

3. Click the right arrow to add space or the left arrow to delete space **(Figures 13, 15a-b)**.

or

Enter a number between -500% and 500% in increments as small as .01 in the Tracking & Kerning field, then press Return.

✔ Tips

■ To kern or track in finer increments, hold down Option while clicking the right or left arrow.

■ Tracking or kerning values can also be applied using the Kern or Track dialog box opened from the Style menu.

Tomorrow

Figure 12. *Click between two characters to kern.*

Figure 13. *The Tracking & Kerning arrows and field on the Measurements palette.*

Tomorrow

Figure 14. *The space between the "T" and the "o" has been reduced.*

C I V I L I Z A T I O N

is the

E N C O U R A G E M E N T

of

D I F F E R E N C E S.

Mohandas Gandhi

Figure 15a. *A phrase with positive tracking values.*

Nothing

great

was

ever

achieved

without

enthusiasm.

Emerson

Figure 15b. *A phrase with a negative tracking value of -6. Positive and negative tracking values can be used to create a variety of typographic effects.*

Tracking and Kerning

To Tr Ta Yo Ya
Wo Wa We Va Vo

Figure 16. *These are some of the character pairs that often need extra kerning, particularly in large point sizes.*

Style is self-plagiarism.

Figure 17a. *A phrase with a normal word space value.*

Style is self-plagiarism.

Alfred Hitchcock

Figure 17b. *The same phrase with a word space value of -10. Negative Word Space Tracking can improve the appearance of headlines and other phrases set in large point sizes.*

Utilities
Check Spelling ▶
Auxiliary Dictionary...
Edit Auxiliary...
Suggested Hyphenation... ⌘H
Hyphenation Exceptions...
Library...
Font Usage...
Picture Usage...
Tracking Edit...
Kerning Table Edit...
Remove Manual Kerning
Alternate Em Spaces

Figure 18. *Select **Remove Manual Kerning** from the **Utilities** menu to restore normal kerning values to highlighted text.*

To kern or track using the keyboard:

1. Select the Content tool.
2. Click between two characters or highlight any number of characters.
3. Hold down Command (⌘) and Shift and press left bracket ([) to delete space, or right bracket (]) to add space.

✔ Tip

■ To kern or track in finer increments, add the Option key to the above keyboard shortcut.

Note: The Word Space Tracking and Remove Manual Kerning commands are included in the FeaturesPlus XTension. They are not part of the QuarkXPress application.

To adjust the space between words only:

1. Select the Content tool.
2. Highlight one or more words.
3. Hold down Command (⌘), Control, Shift and press left bracket ([) to delete space, or right bracket (]) to add space **(Figures 17a-b)**.

✔ Tips

■ Word space tracking can be applied only via the keyboard.

■ To adjust word spacing in finer increments, add the Option key to the above keyboard shortcut.

To remove kerning and Word Space Tracking:

1. Select the Content tool.
2. Highlight the kerned text.
3. Select "Remove Manual Kerning" from the Utilities menu **(Figure 18)**.

✔ Tip

■ The Remove Manual Kerning command does not restore tracking values.

About horizontal scaling:

Normal text has a horizontal scale value of 100%. Horizontal scaling is the extending (widening) or condensing (narrowing) of type. The height of the characters is not affected when horizontal scale values are modified.

To horizontally scale text using the Style menu:

1. Select the Content tool.

2. Highlight the text to be scaled.

3. Select Horizontal Scale from the Style menu **(Figure 19)**.

4. Enter a number between 25% and 99% to condense type (make narrower than normal) or a number between 101% and 400% to expand type (make wider than normal) **(Figures 20-22)**.

5. Click OK or press Return.

To horizontally scale text using the keyboard:

1. Select the Content tool.

2. Highlight the text to be scaled.

3. Hold down Command (⌘) and press left bracket ([) to condense in 5% increments, or right bracket (]) to expand in 5% increments.

Figure 19. *Select* ***Horizontal Scale*** *from the* ***Style*** *menu.*

Figure 20. *The Horizontal Scale feature can be used to stylize type or facilitate copy fitting.*

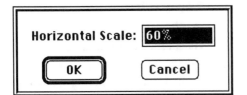

Figure 21. *A value of 60% in the Horizontal Scale dialog box will condense type 40%.*

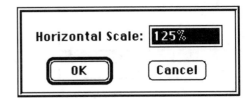

Figure 22. *A value of 125% in the Horizontal Scale dialog box will expand type 25%.*

Horizontal Scaling

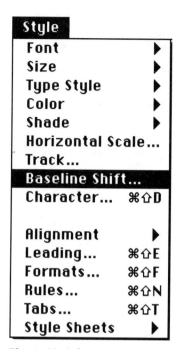

Figure 23. *Select **Baseline Shift** from the **Style** menu.*

Baseline Shift: `-4`

OK   Cancel

Figure 24. *A negative number in the Baseline Shift dialog box will shift the characters below the baseline; a positive number will shift the characters above the baseline.*

About Baseline Shift:

Using the Baseline Shift command, the position of one or more characters can be raised above or lowered below the baseline.

To shift type using the Baseline Shift dialog box:

1. Select the Content tool.
2. Highlight the characters to be shifted.
3. Select Baseline Shift from the Style menu **(Figure 23)**.
4. Enter a number up to three times the point size of the type to be shifted. Insert a minus sign (-) followed by a number to shift the type below the baseline **(Figures 24-26)**.
5. Click OK or press Return.

To shift type using the keyboard:

1. Select the Content tool.
2. Highlight the characters to be shifted.
3. Hold down Command (⌘), Option, Shift and press hyphen (-) to lower the type below the baseline, or plus sign (+) to raise the type above the baseline in 1 point increments.

Baseline Shift

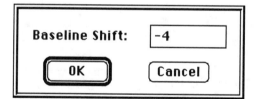

Figure 25. *In this example, some characters have been shifted above the baseline and some have been shifted below the baseline.*

Figure 26. *The Baseline Shift feature is useful for creating logos and other special type configurations.*

About Key Caps:

Key Caps is an Apple Menu item that displays keystroke combinations for producing special characters.

To use Key Caps:

1. Select Key Caps from the Apple menu.

2. Select a font from the Key Caps menu.

3. Look at the keyboard diagram as you hold down Option or Option and Shift together. Make a note of the keystroke combination that produces the desired special character **(Figure 27)**.

4. Select Quit from the File menu.

5. If not already selected, select the correct font for the special character keystroke combination.

6. Enter the keystroke combination into your text.

A few special characters and their corresponding keystroke combinations.

"	Option [
"	Option Shift [
'	Option]
'	Option Shift]
•	Option 8
©	Option g
®	Option r
é	Option e, e again
¢	Option 4
—	Option Shift hyphen (em dash)
–	Option hyphen (en dash)
/	Option Shift 1
°	Option Shift 8

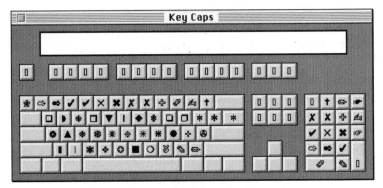

Figure 27. *The Key Caps utility displays special character sets.*

To insert one Zapf Dingbat character:

1. Select the Content tool.

2. Click in a line of text to create an insertion point.

3. Hold down Command (⌘) and Shift and press "Z."

4. Press any key or keyboard combination to produce the desired Zapf Dingbat character **(Figure 28)**.

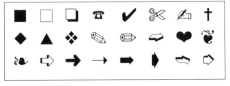

Figure 28. *A few Zapf Dingbats characters.*

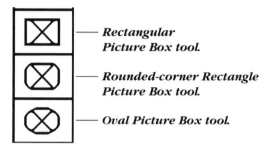

Figure 1. *Three of the Picture Box tools.*

— *Rectangular Picture Box tool.*

— *Rounded-corner Rectangle Picture Box tool.*

— *Oval Picture Box tool.*

About Pictures:

In QuarkXPress, pictures can be imported into various-shaped picture boxes. File formats that can be imported include TIFF, RIFF, PAINT, PICT, and EPS.

To create a picture box:

1. Select any of the first three Picture Box tools. The cursor will temporarily turn into a crosshair icon **(Figure 1)**.

2. Press and drag in any direction **(Figures 2a-b)**.

(See Create a Polygon in this chapter)

✔ Tip

■ Hold down Shift and press and drag a handle to reshape a rectangular picture box into a square or an oval picture box into a circle. This tip also applies to text boxes.

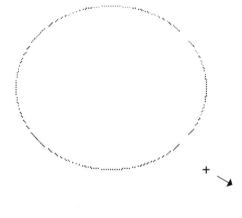

Figure 2a. *Press and drag to create a picture box.*

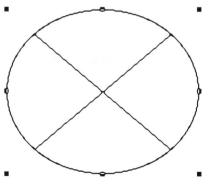

Figure 2b. *An empty picture box has an "x" through its center.*

Create a Picture Box

To resize a picture box manually:

1. Select the Item or Content tool.

2. Click on a picture box.

3. Press and drag any handle **(Figures 3-4)**.

✔ Tip

■ Hold down Option and Shift while dragging to preserve the original proportions of the box.

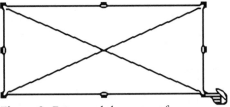

Figure 3. *Press and drag any of the four corner handles of a box.*

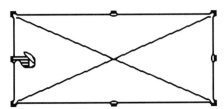

Figure 4. *Press and drag any of the four midpoint handles of a box.*

To resize a picture box using the Measurements palette:

1. Select the Item or Content tool.

2. Click on a picture box.

3. Next to the W in the Measurements palette, enter a number in increments as small as .001 to modify the width of the box **(Figure 5)**.

and/or

Next to the H in the Measurements palette, enter a number to modify the height of the box.

4. Press Return.

✔ Tip

■ To enlarge or reduce the dimensions of a box by a specified amount, insert the cursor after the current value in the W or H field, enter a plus (+) or minus (-) sign, then enter an additional value in any measurement system used in QuarkXPress.

*The **Width** field with two inches added to the existing four pica width of a box.*

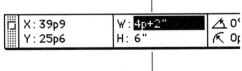

*The **Height** of a box.*

Figure 5. *The Width and Height can be entered in any of the measurement systems used in QuarkXPress.*

Item

Modify...	⌘M
Frame...	⌘B
Runaround...	⌘T
Duplicate	⌘D
Step and Repeat...	
Delete	⌘K
Group	⌘G
Ungroup	⌘U
Constrain	
Lock	⌘L
Send to Back	
Bring to Front	
Space/Align...	
Picture Box Shape	▶
Reshape Polygon	

Figure 6. *Click on a picture box, then select* **Delete** *from the* **Item** *menu.*

To delete a picture box:

1. Select the Item or Content tool.

2. Click on a picture box.

3. Select Delete from the Item menu **(Figure 6)**.
or
Hold down Command and press "K".

✔ Tip

■ A picture box selected with the Item tool can also be deleted by pressing Delete on the keyboard or selecting Clear from the Edit menu.

To move a picture box manually:

1. Select the Item tool.

2. Press on the inside of a picture box, pause briefly for the picture to redraw, then drag in any direction **(Figures 7a-b)**.

✔ Tip

■ A picture box, as well as any other item, can be dragged from one page to another.

■ If you do not pause before dragging, only the outline of the box will be displayed as it is moved.

The clock icon appears while the picture is redrawing.

Figure 7a. *Press, then pause before dragging to display the picture as it is moved.*

Figure 7b. *The Item tool icon appears when the picture is ready to be dragged.*

To reposition a picture box using the Measurements palette:

1. Select the Item or Content tool.

2. Click on a picture box.

3. Enter a number in the X field on the Measurements palette to modify the horizontal position of the box relative to the ruler origin **(Figure 8)**. *and/or*
Enter a number in the Y field to modify the vertical position.

4. Press Return.

✔ Tip

■ To move a box a specified amount horizontally or vertically, insert the cursor after the number in the X or Y field, enter a plus (+) or minus (-) sign, and then enter a number in any measurements system used in QuarkXPress **(Figures 9a-b)**.

*The **horizontal** position of a picture box.*

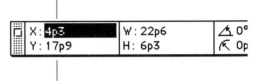

*The **vertical** position of a picture box.*

Figure 8. *The Measurements palette.*

Figure 9a. *Add a positive or negative number to the right of the number in the X or Y field, then press Return.*

| | X: 4p3 +3p | W: 19p1.744 | △ 0° |
| | Y: 44p1 | H: 3p9 | ⏋ 0p |

| | X: 7p3 | W: 2p.786 | △ 0° |
| | Y: 39p1.542 | H: 1p6.724 | ⏋ 0p |

Figure 9b. *The two numbers are added together, causing the box to be repositioned.*

To create a bleed:

To create a bleed, position any item (picture box, text box, or line) so that part of the item is on the page and part of the item is on the pasteboard **(Figure 10)**. An item that is completely on the pasteboard will not print.

✔ Tip

■ Check the Registration Marks box in the Print dialog box to increase the print area around the page.

(See Chapter 17, Printing)

Figure 10. *Items positioned to create a "bleed."*

Figure 11a. *Press and drag from a ruler to place a ruler guide on a document page.*

Figure 11b. *An item snaps to a guide when dragged within the specified Snap Distance of the guide.*

About Ruler Guides:

Ruler guides can be dragged from the horizontal or vertical ruler onto the document page to aid in the layout process. If Snap to Guides is turned on from the View menu, an item that is moved near a guide will "snap" to the guide if it is within the distance specified in the Snap Distance field in the General Preferences dialog box. The default Snap Distance is 6 pixels.

To position a box using a ruler guide:

1. Press and drag a guide from the horizontal or vertical ruler onto the document page. As you drag, the position of the guide will be indicated by a marker on the ruler and in the X or Y field on the Measurements palette **(Figure 11a)**.

2. Press and drag an item to the guide. The item will "snap" to the guide if Snap to Guides is on **(Figure 11b)**.

✔ Tips

■ To remove a ruler guide from a page, select the Item tool and drag the guide back onto the ruler.

■ To remove all the horizontal or vertical guides at one time, make sure there is no pasteboard showing between the edge of the page and the corresponding ruler, then hold down Option and click on the horizontal ruler to remove all the horizontal guides, or the vertical ruler to remove all the vertical guides.

■ Ruler guides are displayed in front of page elements or behind page elements depending on whether In Front or Behind is selected from the Guides pop-up menu in the General Preferences dialog box, opened from the Edit menu. Ruler guides do not print.

Use a Guide to Position a Box

About importing pictures:

When a picture is imported into a picture box, a screen version of it is saved with the QuarkXPress file for display purposes. Also saved with the QuarkXPress file is information about changes made within the QuarkXPress file, such as cropping, rotating, or scaling. The original picture file is not modified by such changes. A path is created to the original picture file, which the QuarkXPress file accesses when the document is printed.
(See Update a Picture in this chapter)

To import a picture:

1. Select the Content tool.

2. Click on a picture box.

3. Select Get Picture from the File menu **(Figure 12)**.
or
Hold down Command (⌘) and press "E".

4. Select a picture file and click Open **(Figure 13)**
or
Double-click a picture file.

Select a picture file.

File

New...	⌘N
Open...	⌘O
Close	
Save	⌘S
Save as...	
Revert to Saved	
Get Picture...	**⌘E**
Save Text...	
Save Page as EPS...	
Document Setup...	
Page Setup...	
Print...	⌘P
Quit	⌘Q

Figure 12. *Select **Get Picture** from the **File** menu.*

Figure 13. *The Get Picture dialog box.*

*With the **Picture Preview** box checked, a preview of the currently selected file is displayed.*

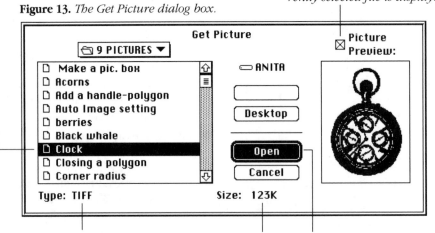

*The picture file **Type**. Quark imports PAINT, PICT, EPS, TIFF and RIFF pictures.*

*The picture **Size**. Click **Open** to import.*

Import a Picture

Horizontal scale of a picture.

X% : 50%	◁▷ X+ : 0p
Y% : 100%	⇕ Y+ : 0p

Vertical scale of a picture.

Figure 14. *When the X and Y percentages differ from each other, a picture's proportions have been altered relative to the original.*

X% : 75%	◁▷ X+ : p5.438
Y% : 75%	⇕ Y+ : p2.472

Figure 15. *When the X and Y percentages match, a picture's proportions have been preserved relative to the original.*

Figure 16. *A picture with an X coordinate of 55% and a Y coordinate of 55%.*

Figure 17. *A picture with an X coordinate of 70% and a Y coordinate of 50%.*

To resize a picture:

1. Select the Content tool.

2. Click on a picture.

3. Hold down Command (⌘), Option, Shift and press the > key to enlarge the picture or the < key to reduce the picture in 5% increments.

or

Enter numbers in the X% and/or Y% picture size fields in the Measurements palette, then press Return **(Figures 14-18)**.

✔ Tip

■ The percentages in the size fields in the Measurements palette can be supplied as "For Position Only" information to a printer for traditional stripping. These numbers can be used for a scanned picture only if the original was scanned at 100%.

Figure 18. *A picture with an X coordinate of 50% and a Y coordinate of 70%.*

Resize a Picture

Resize a Picture

Additional keystrokes for resizing pictures.

To fit a picture into its box:

1. Select the Content tool.

2. Click on a picture.

3. Hold down Command (⌘), Option, Shift and press "F" **(Figures 19a-b)**.

✔ Tip

■ If the Option key is not included in the above keystroke, the picture will fit into its box, but its proportions will be altered relative to the original **(Figure 19c)**.

Figure 19a. *A picture before being resized.*

To resize a picture and its box simultaneously:

1. Select the Content tool.

2. Hold down Command (⌘), Option, Shift, pause briefly for the picture to redraw, then press and drag any handle **(Figure 20)**.

Figure 19b. *A picture after the* **Command, Option, Shift/F** *keystroke has been applied.*

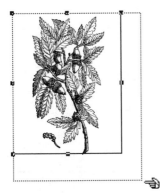

Figure 20. *Hold down* **Command, Option, Shift** *and press and drag a handle to resize a picture and its box simultaneously.*

Figure 19c. *A picture after the* **Command, Shift/F** *keystroke has been applied.*

Figure 21. *A picture being moved within its box. Note the hand icon.*

To crop a picture by moving it within its box:

1. Select the Content tool.

2. Press on a picture, pause briefly until the hand icon appears, then drag **(Figure 21)**.

✔ Tip

- Click on a picture and press any of the four arrow keys on the keyboard to move a picture in 1 point increments. Hold down Option and press any of the arrow keys to move a picture in .1 point increments.

To crop a picture by resizing its box:

1. Select the Item or Content tool.

2. Press and drag any handle of a picture box **(Figures 22a-b)**.

To delete a picture:

1. Select the Content tool.

2. Click on a picture.

3. Press Delete.

Figure 22a. *Press and drag any handle to crop a picture.*

Figure 22b. *After cropping.*

To convert a picture box shape:

1. Select the Item or Content tool.

2. Click on a picture box.

3. Select any shape from the six selections in the Picture Box Shape pop-up menu under the Item menu **(Figures 23-24b)**.

Figure 23. *A picture box can be converted into any of the other shapes found under the **Picture Box Shape** pop-up menu.*

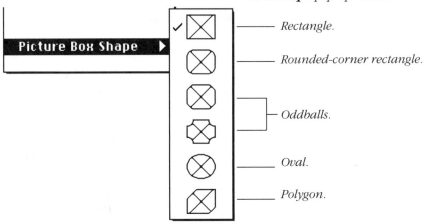

Rectangle.

Rounded-corner rectangle.

Oddballs.

Oval.

Polygon.

Figure 24a. *A rectangular picture box...*

Figure 24b. *...converted into an "oddball."*

To modify the corners of a picture box:

Enter a number in the corner radius field in the Measurements palette to modify the amount of curve of the corners of a rectangle, rounded-corner rectangle or "oddball" shape **(Figure 25)**.

Figure 25. *In the corner radius field on the Measurements palette, enter a number between 0" and 2" in any measurement system used in QuarkXPress.*

To rotate a picture and its box using the Measurements palette:

1. Select the Item or Content tool.

2. Click on a picture box.

3. In the picture and box angle field on the left side of the Measurements palette, enter a positive number to rotate counterclockwise or a negative number to rotate clockwise between 360° and 360° in increments as small as .001° **(Figure 26)**.

4. Press Return.

*The **picture and box angle** field.*

| X: 4p7.731 | W: 33p4.269 | ⚓ 0° | X%: 100% | ⬦⬦ X+: 0p | ⚓ 20° |
| Y: 22p.531 | H: 3p2.114 | ⟋ 0p | Y%: 100% | ⬦ Y+: 0p | ⟋ 0° |

Figure 26. *The Measurements palette.*

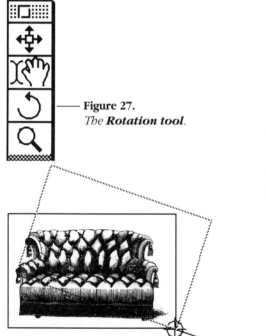

Figure 27.
*The **Rotation tool**.*

To rotate a picture and its box using the Rotation tool:

1. Select the Rotation tool **(Figure 27)**.

2. Click on a picture box.

3. Press to create an anchor point, pause briefly for the picture to redraw, then drag away from the anchor point to create a "lever" **(Figure 28)**.

4. Drag the "lever" clockwise or counterclockwise **(Figure 29)**.

✔ Tip

■ Hold down Shift while dragging with the Rotation tool to rotate an item in 45° increments.

Figure 28. *If you drag away from the axis point before rotating, you will create a "lever," and the rotation will be easier to control. If you do not pause before dragging, only the outline of the box will be displayed as it is being rotated.*

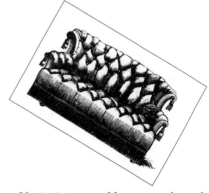

Figure 29. *A picture and box rotated together.*

To rotate a picture alone:

1. Select the Content tool.

2. Click on a picture.

3. In the picture angle field on the right side of the Measurements palette, enter a positive number to rotate counterclockwise or a negative number to rotate clockwise **(Figure 30)**.

4. Press Return **(Figures 31-34)**.

✔ Tip

■ To rotate the picture box and **not** the picture, first rotate the box with the picture, then rotate the picture alone the negative amount. For example, if the picture with its box is rotated 20°, rotate the picture back -20°.

Figure 30. *The* **picture angle** *field.*

X: 4p7.731	W: 33p4.269	△ 0°	X%: 100%	◇▷ X+: 0p		△ 20°
Y: 22p.531	H: 3p2.114	⟨ 0p	Y%: 100%	⇕ Y+: 0p		⟋ 0°

Figure 31. *0° rotation.*

Figure 32. *180° rotation.*

Figure 33. *90° rotation.*

Figure 34. *40° rotation.*

Item	
Modify...	⌘M
Frame...	⌘B
Runaround...	⌘T
Duplicate	⌘D
Step and Repeat...	
Delete	⌘K
Group	⌘G
Ungroup	⌘U
Constrain	
Lock	⌘L
Send to Back	
Bring to Front	
Space/Align...	
Picture Box Shape	▶
Reshape Polygon	

Figure 35. *Select **Frame** from the **Item** menu.*

To frame a picture box:

1. Select the Item or Content tool.

2. Click on a box.

3. Select Frame from the Item menu **(Figure 35)**.
or
Hold down Command (⌘) and press "B".

4. Select a preset width from the Width pop-up menu **(Figure 36)**.
or
Enter a custom width between .001 and 504 points in the Width field.

Steps 5-7 are optional.

5. Select an alternate frame Style. The non-straight line styles can only be applied to a rectangular box.

6. Select a color from the Color pop-up menu.

7. Select a shade from the Shade pop-up menu, or enter a percentage in the Shade field.

8. Click OK or press Return.
(See page 43 for an illustration of various frames)

Figure 36. *The Frame Specifications dialog box.*

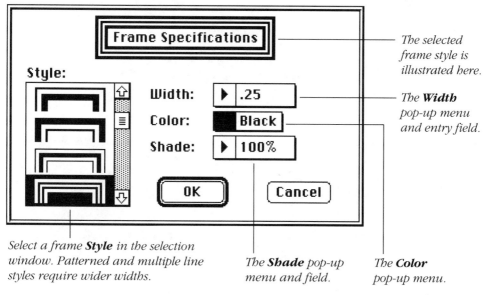

The selected frame style is illustrated here.

*The **Width** pop-up menu and entry field.*

*Select a frame **Style** in the selection window. Patterned and multiple line styles require wider widths.*

*The **Shade** pop-up menu and field.*

*The **Color** pop-up menu.*

Frame a Picture Box

To convert any picture box into a polygon picture box:

1. Click on a picture box of any shape.

2. Select the polygon icon from the Picture Box Shape pop-up menu under the Item menu **(Figure 37)**.

To create a polygon picture box using the Polygon tool:

1. Select the Polygon tool from the tool palette **(Figure 38)**.

2. Click once to establish a starting point.

3. Move the mouse and click to create a second handle. Repeat to create at least one more handle.

4. Close the polygon by clicking on the starting point.

   or

   Double-click anywhere **(Figures 39a-d)**.

✔ Tips

■ Hold down Command (⌘) and press Period (.) to delete an unfinished polygon.

■ A polygon or oval picture box with a Background of None may not print.

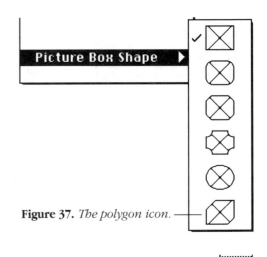

Figure 37. *The polygon icon.*

Figure 38. *Select the* **Polygon Picture Box tool.**

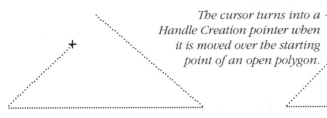

The cursor turns into a Handle Creation pointer when it is moved over the starting point of an open polygon.

Figure 39a. *Click to create handles.*

Figure 39b. *Be sure to close up the polygon, or it will run wild!*

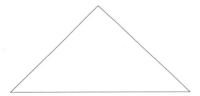

Figure 39c. *The completed polygon.*

Figure 39d. *A polygon with a picture.*

Create a Polygon

Item	
Modify...	⌘M
Frame...	⌘B
Runaround...	⌘T
Duplicate	⌘D
Step and Repeat...	
Delete	⌘K
Group	⌘G
Ungroup	⌘U
Constrain	
Lock	⌘L
Send to Back	
Bring to Front	
Space/Align...	
Picture Box Shape	▶
Reshape Polygon	

Figure 40.
*To modify a polygon, first select **Reshape Polygon** from the **Item** menu.*

Before reshaping a polygon:

1. Select the Item or Content tool.

2. Click on a polygon.

3. Select Reshape Polygon from the Item menu **(Figure 40)**.

To reshape a polygon:

1. Select the Item or Content tool.

2. Click on a polygon.

3. Press and drag a handle or line segment **(Figure 41)**.

or

Add a handle by holding down Command (⌘), moving the cursor over a line segment, then clicking when the cursor turns into a Handle Creation pointer **(Figure 42)**.

or

Delete a handle by holding down Command (⌘), moving the cursor over a handle, then clicking when the cursor turns into a Handle Deletion pointer **(Figure 43)**.

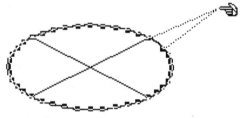

Figure 41. *Press and drag a handle or line segment to reshape a polygon.*

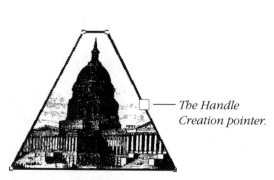

Figure 42. *To add a handle, hold down* **Command** *(⌘) and click on a line segment.*

The Handle Creation pointer.

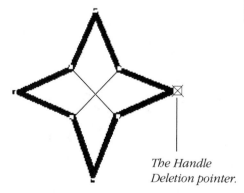

The Handle Deletion pointer.

Figure 43. *To delete a handle, hold down* **Command** *(⌘) and click on it.*

Reshape a Polygon

About picture styling:

A few of the basic picture modifications, such as posterization or contrast modification, that can be accomplished within QuarkXPress are outlined here. An application solely dedicated to image manipulation should be used for elaborate masking, filtering, or retouching. Keep in mind that modifications made to a picture in QuarkXPress do not affect the original picture file. *(See also Chapter 13, Apply Color)*

To posterize a picture:

1. Select the Content tool.

2. Click on a color bitmap, color or gray-scale TIFF, or grayscale RIFF picture.

3. Select Posterized from the Style menu **(Figure 44-46)**.

✔ Tip

■ To restore a picture's contrast values, select the Content tool and click on the picture, then select Normal Contrast from the Style menu.

To apply a shade to a picture:

1. Select the Content tool.

2. Click on a black & white bitmap or a TIFF or RIFF line art picture.

3. Select a preset shade from the Shade pop-up menu under the Style menu.
or
Select Other from the same menu, enter a custom percentage, then click OK **(Figures 44 and 47)**.

Figure 47. *A TIFF line art picture with a 30% shade.*

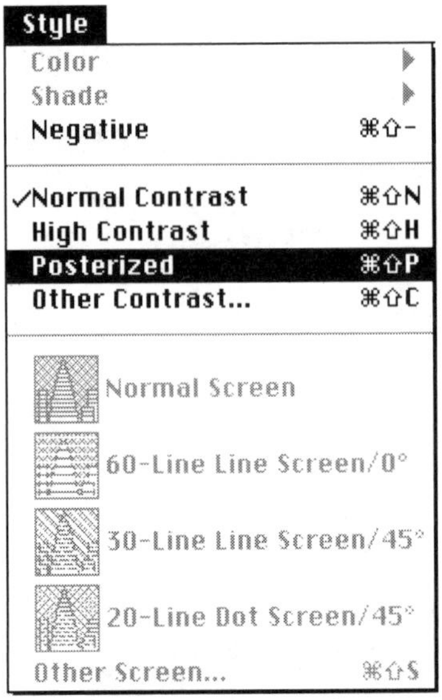

Figure 44. *Select a contrast option from the **Style** menu.*

Figure 45.
Normal Contrast.

Don Snyder Photography Inc.

Figure 46. *Posterization reduces the number of grays in a picture to black, white and four gray levels in between.*

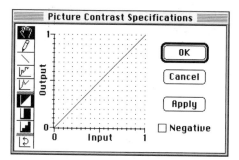

Figure 48a. *The normal contrast setting for a grayscale picture.*

To apply a custom contrast setting to a grayscale picture:

1. Select the Content tool.

2. Click on a grayscale TIFF or RIFF picture.

3. Select Other Contrast from the Style menu **(Figure 44)**.

4. Select the hand tool in the Picture Contrast Specifications dialog box and drag the contrast curve in any direction. Move it downward and to the right to lighten the picture **(Figures 48a-c)**.
or
Select the pencil tool in the Picture Contrast Specifications dialog box and draw a custom curve **(Figures 49a-b)**.

6. Click Apply to preview.

7. Click OK or press Return.

✔ Tip

■ The contrast setting can also be adjusted for a color bitmap or TIFF picture.

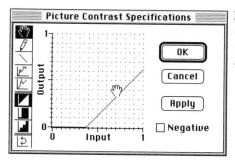

Figure 48b. *The contrast curve moved with the hand tool.*

Figure 48c. *A picture with the contrast curve shown in Figure 48b.*

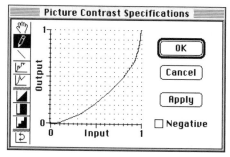

Figure 49a. *A custom contrast curve drawn with the pencil tool.*

Figure 49b. *A picture with the contrast curve shown in Figure 49a.*

Style a Picture

About saving a page as an EPS:

A QuarkXPress page can be converted into a picture file using the Save Page as EPS command. This feature can be used to create special drop caps to which Auto or Manual Image Runaround can be applied, to create words that can be cropped, or to place a page within a page. An EPS file cannot be edited, so be sure to save the file from which it is generated so that you will have the option to generate another EPS file from it later **(Figures 52-55)**.

(See Wrap Text Around a Picture in this chapter)

To save a page as an EPS file:

1. Create or open a file that contains a page that you would like to save as an EPS file.

2. Select Save Page as EPS from the File menu **(Figure 50)**.

3. Enter a name for the EPS file in the Save page as field **(Figure 51)**.

4. Enter the number of the page to be saved as EPS in the Page field.

5. Enter a percentage between 10% and 100% in the Scale field.

6. Click Color or Black & White.

7. Click Save.

✔ Tips

■ When an EPS containing text is imported into a QuarkXPress file, the corresponding printer fonts must be available in the system for the EPS to print properly.

■ An EPS file should not be imported into another EPS file.

■ The OPI options are used for creating color separations.

Figure 50. *Select **Save Page as EPS** from the **File** menu.*

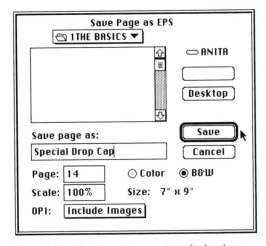

Figure 51. *The Save Page as EPS dialog box.*

(sidebar) **Save a Page as an EPS**

Whale

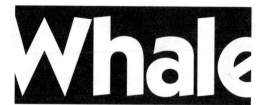

Figure 52. *A file containing this word was saved as an EPS file and then imported into a picture box so that it could be cropped.*

Whale

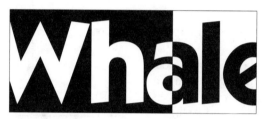

Figure 53. *This compound word was created by placing two picture boxes, each containing an EPS file, side-by-side.*

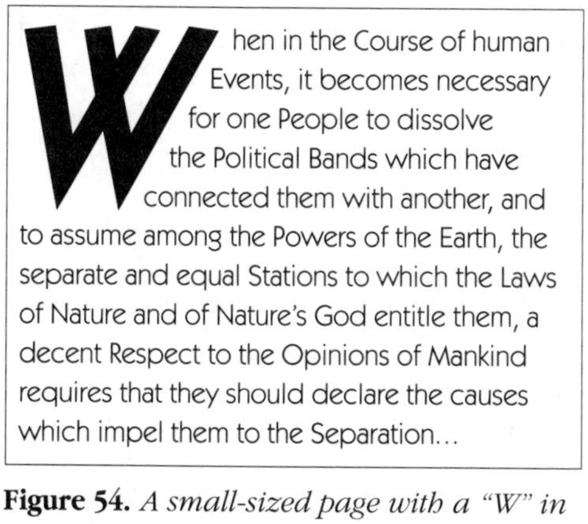

When in the Course of human Events, it becomes necessary for one People to dissolve the Political Bands which have connected them with another, and to assume among the Powers of the Earth, the separate and equal Stations to which the Laws of Nature and of Nature's God entitle them, a decent Respect to the Opinions of Mankind requires that they should declare the causes which impel them to the Separation…

Figure 54. *A small-sized page with a "W" in a text box was saved as an EPS file and then imported into a picture box. The Auto Image Runaround option was applied to the picture to cause the surrounding text to wrap around the contour of the "W."*

Chapter 7 Paragraph Formatting

To "break" a line without creating a new paragraph:

1. Select the Content tool.
2. Click in the text where a line break is to occur.
3. Hold down Shift and press Return. With Invisibles on, a Shift-Return is displayed as a left-pointing arrow icon **(Figures 17-19)**.

✓ Tips

- To remove a line break command, or "soft return," click at the beginning of the next line and press Delete.
- This command can be used to adjust headlines or fix awkward breaks in ragged right copy.

Figure 17. *This is an awkward break.*

The night so luminous on the spar-deck, but otherwise on the cavernous ones below — levels so very like the tiered galleries in a coal-mine — the luminous night passed away. Like the prophet in the chariot disappearing in heaven and dropping his mantle to Elisha, the withdrawing night transferred its pale robe to the peeping day.

The night so luminous on the spar-deck, but otherwise on the cavernous ones below — levels so very like the tiered¶

galleries in a coal-mine — the luminous night passed away. Like the prophet in the chariot disappearing in heaven and dropping his mantle to Elisha, the withdrawing night transferred its pale robe to the peeping day.

Figure 18. *A paragraph return creates a new paragraph.*

The night so luminous on the spar-deck, but otherwise on the cavernous ones below — levels so very like the tiered ↵
galleries in a coal-mine — the luminous night passed away. Like the prophet in the chariot disappearing in heaven and dropping his mantle to Elisha, the withdrawing night transferred its pale robe to the peeping day.

Herman Melville

Figure 19. *A* ***Shift-Return*** *creates a new line within a paragraph.*

A quick way to copy paragraph formats from one paragraph to another within a story.
Click in a paragraph or press and drag through a series of paragraphs that are to be modified. Hold down Option and Shift and click in the paragraph whose formats you would like to copy.

Insert a Line Break

70

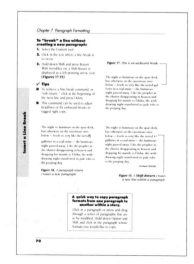

Figure 55. *A page-within-a-page. This is page 70 of this book, saved as an EPS file, then imported into a picture box.*

Wrap Text Around a Box

About the Runaround feature:

There are several ways to combine text and pictures. For example, text can wrap around the irregular contours of a picture or around a picture box, or a picture can be placed behind a transparent text box.

To wrap text around a picture box:

1. Select the Item or Content tool.

2. Select a picture box.

3. Select Runaround from the Item menu **(Figure 56)**.

4. Select Item from the Mode pop-up menu **(Figure 57)**.

5. To adjust the space between each side of a rectangular picture box and the text wrapping around it, enter numbers in the Top, Left, Bottom, and Right fields. If any other picture box shape is selected, enter a single number in the Text Outset field.

6. Click OK or press Return **(Figure 58)**.

✔ Tip

■ The picture box must be on top of the text box for Runaround to work. If necessary, select the picture box and select Bring to Front from the Item menu.

Figure 56. *Select **Runaround** from the **Item** menu.*

Item	
Modify...	⌘M
Frame...	⌘B
Runaround...	**⌘T**
Duplicate	⌘D
Step and Repeat...	
Delete	⌘K
Group	⌘G
Ungroup	⌘U
Constrain	
Lock	⌘L
Send to Back	
Bring to Front	
Space/Align...	
Picture Box Shape	▶
Reshape Polygon	

Runaround Specifications

Mode: [Item]

Top: [12 pt] ☐

Left: [8 pt]

Bottom: [10 pt] [OK]

Right: [12 pt] [Cancel]

Figure 57. *Select **Item** from the **Mode** pop-up menu.*

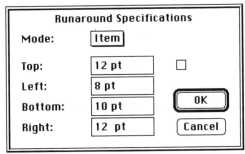

With my aversion to this cat, however, its partiality for myself seemed to increase. It followed my footsteps with a pertinacity which it would be difficult to make the reader comprehend. Whenever I sat, it would crouch beneath my chair, or spring upon my knees, covering me with its loathsome caresses. If I arose to walk it would get between my feet and thus nearly throw me down, or, fastening its long and sharp claws in my dress, clamber, in this manner to, to my breast. At such times, although I longed to destroy it with a blow, I was yet withheld from so doing, partly by a memory of my former crime, but chiefly—let me confess it at once—by absolute *dread* of the beast...

Edgar Allan Poe

Figure 58. *Text will only wrap around three sides of a box that is placed within a column. Text will wrap around all four sides of a box if it straddles two columns, as in this example.*

Runaround Specifications

Mode: **Auto Image**

Text Outset: 6 pt ☐

Left:

Bottom:

Right:

[OK]

[Cancel]

Figure 59. *Select **Auto Image** from the **Mode** pop-up menu.*

To wrap text around a picture:

1. Select the Item or Content tool.

2. Select a picture box.

3. Select Runaround from the Item menu **(Figure 56)**.

4. Select Auto Image from the Mode pop-up menu **(Figure 59)**.

5. Enter a number in points in the Text Outset field to adjust the space between the picture and the surrounding text.

6. Click OK or press Return.

7. Deselect the picture and text box by clicking in the margin or pasteboard to make the screen redraw **(Figure 60)**.

✔ Tip

■ For Auto Image to work properly, as in Figure 60, a picture with an irregular contour silhouetted on a white background should be chosen.

"Then, pray tell me what it is that you can infer from this hat?"

He picked it up and gazed at it in the peculiar introspective fashion which was characteristic of him. "It is perhaps less suggestive than it might have been," he remarked, "and yet there are a few inferences which are very distinct, and a few others which represent at least a strong balance of probability. That the man was highly intellectual is of course obvious upon the face of it, and also that he was fairly well-to-do within the last three years, although he has now fallen upon evil days. He had foresight, but has less now than formerly, pointing to a moral retrogression, which, when taken with the decline of his fortunes, seems to indicate some evil influence, probably drink, at work upon him. This may account also for the obvious fact that his wife has ceased to love him..."

Sir Arthur Conan Doyle

Figure 60. *Auto Image Runaround.*

About Manual Image:

When Manual Image Runaround mode is selected for a picture, a second set of handles called the Runaround polygon appears around it. The text wrap around a picture can be customized by modifying the Runaround polygon.

To create a Runaround polygon:

1. Select the Item or Content tool.

2. Select a picture box.

3. Select Runaround from the Item menu **(Figure 61)**.

4. Select Manual Image from the Mode pop-up menu **(Figure 62)**.

5. Enter a number in the Text Outset field to adjust the space between the Runaround polygon and the surrounding text.

6. Click OK or press Return **(Figure 64)**.

7. Deselect the picture and text box by clicking in the margin or pasteboard to make the screen redraw.

To reshape a Runaround polygon:

Press and drag a handle or line segment **(Figure 65)**.

or

Add a handle by holding down Command (⌘), moving the cursor over a line segment, and clicking when the cursor turns into a Handle Creation pointer **(Figure 66)**.

or

Delete a handle by holding down Command (⌘), moving the cursor over a handle, and clicking when the cursor turns into a Handle Deletion pointer **(Figure 67)**.

✔ Tip

■ Hold down the Space bar while reshaping a polygon to prevent the surrounding text from reflowing. The text will reflow when the Space bar is released.

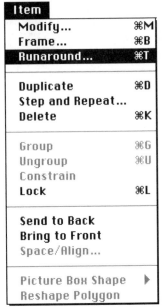

Figure 61. *Select **Runaround** from the **Item** menu.*

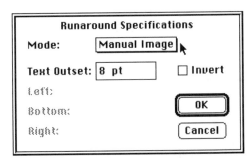

Figure 62. *Select **Manual Image** from the **Mode** pop-up menu.*

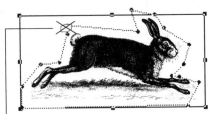

Figure 63. *To change the Runaround setting of a picture from Manual Image to None quickly, hold down Command (⌘) and Shift and click on a handle or line segment when the Polygon Deletion pointer is displayed.*

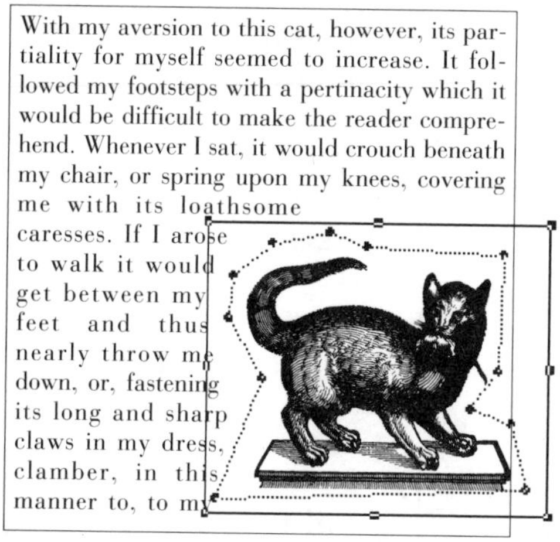

With my aversion to this cat, however, its partiality for myself seemed to increase. It followed my footsteps with a pertinacity which it would be difficult to make the reader comprehend. Whenever I sat, it would crouch beneath my chair, or spring upon my knees, covering me with its loathsome caresses. If I arose to walk it would get between my feet and thus nearly throw me down, or, fastening its long and sharp claws in my dress, clamber, in this manner to, to m

Figure 64. *When the Manual Image option is selected for a picture, a second set of handles called the Runaround polygon appears.*

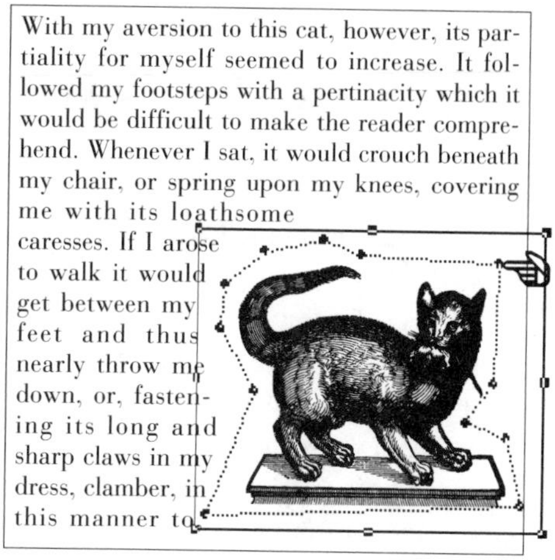

With my aversion to this cat, however, its partiality for myself seemed to increase. It followed my footsteps with a pertinacity which it would be difficult to make the reader comprehend. Whenever I sat, it would crouch beneath my chair, or spring upon my knees, covering me with its loathsome caresses. If I arose to walk it would get between my feet and thus nearly throw me down, or, fastening its long and sharp claws in my dress, clamber, in this manner to

Figure 65. *Press and drag a line segment or handle to reshape a Runaround polygon.*

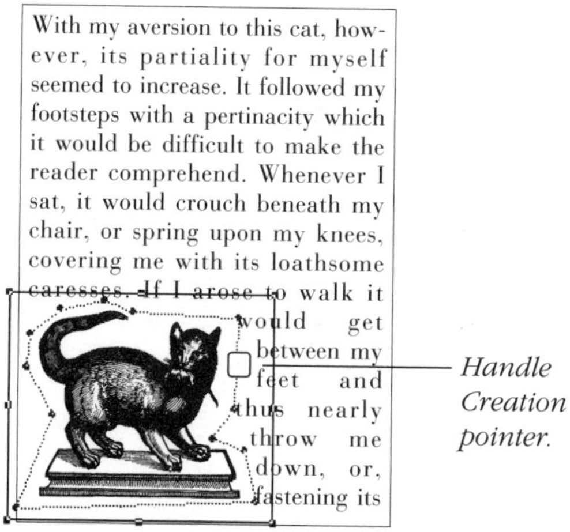

With my aversion to this cat, however, its partiality for myself seemed to increase. It followed my footsteps with a pertinacity which it would be difficult to make the reader comprehend. Whenever I sat, it would crouch beneath my chair, or spring upon my knees, covering me with its loathsome caresses. If I arose to walk it would get between my feet and thus nearly throw me down, or, fastening its

Handle Creation pointer.

Figure 66. *Hold down Command (⌘) and click on a line segment to add a handle.*

With my aversion to this cat, however, its partiality for myself seemed to increase. It followed my footsteps with a pertinacity which it would be difficult to make the reader comprehend. Whenever I sat, it would crouch beneath my chair, or spring upon my knees, covering me with its loathsome caresses. If I arose to walk it would get between my feet and thus nearly throw me down, or, fastening its long

Handle Deletion pointer.

Figure 67. *Hold down Command (⌘) and click on a handle to delete it.*

For a picture to be visible behind a text box, the background of the text box must be transparent.

To layer a picture behind text:

1. Select the Item or Content tool.

2. Select a text box.

3. Select Modify from the Item menu **(Figure 68)**.

4. Select None from the Background pop-up menu. Do not select Black with a shade of 0% **(Figure 69)**.

5. Click OK or press Return.

6. With the text box still selected, select Bring to Front from the Item menu.

7. Deselect the picture and text box by clicking in the margin or pasteboard to make the screen redraw **(Figure 70)**.

✔ Tip

■ Apply a light color tint or shade of gray to the picture so the text will be legible.

(See also Chapter 15, Layer Items)

Layer a Picture Behind Text

Item	
Modify...	⌘M
Frame...	⌘B
Runaround...	⌘T
Duplicate	⌘D
Step and Repeat...	
Delete	⌘K
Group	⌘G
Ungroup	⌘U
Constrain	
Lock	⌘L
Send to Back	
Bring to Front	
Space/Align...	
Picture Box Shape	▶
Reshape Polygon	

Figure 68. *Select **Modify** from the **Item** menu.*

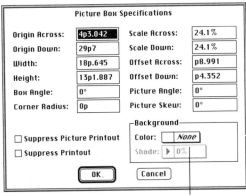

Figure 69. *Select a **Background** color of **None** to make the text box transparent.*

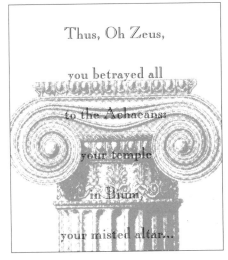

Figure 70. *A shade of 30% was applied to this line art TIFF picture.*

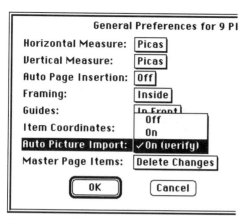

Figure 71. *Select one of three **Auto Picture Import** options in the General Preferences dialog box.*

Figure 72. *Select a picture file, then click **Update**.*

Figure 73. *Click OK or press Return.*

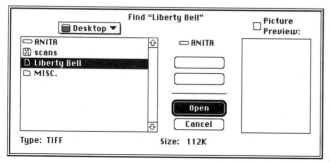

Figure 74. *Select the picture file, then click **Open**.*

The Auto Picture Import options:

When a picture is imported into a QuarkXPress file, information as to the original picture file's name and location is stored in the QuarkXPress file. If the original picture file is modified, renamed or moved, its path to the QuarkXPress file must be updated to print properly.
(See "About importing pictures" in this chapter)

To update the path to a picture when opening a file:

Upon opening a QuarkXPress file, there are three options for updating a modified or missing Picture file. They are available in the Auto Picture Import pop-up menu in the General Preferences dialog box, opened from the Edit menu. If **Off** is selected, the path will not be updated; if **On** is selected, the path will be updated automatically; if **On (verify)** is selected, the Missing/Modified Pictures dialog box will open **(Figure 71)**.

If **On (verify)** is selected, do the following:

1. Click OK if the warning prompt appears.

2. Select a picture file in the Missing/Modified Pictures dialog box **(Figure 72)**.

3. If the "OK to update..." prompt appears, click OK to update a modified picture **(Figure 73)**.
or
Click Update to update a missing picture file, locate and select the picture in the "Find..." dialog box, then click Open **(Figure 74)**.

Update a Picture

The path to a picture file can be updated at any time using the Picture Usage dialog box.

To update the path to a picture using Picture Usage:

1. Select Picture Usage from the Utilities menu **(Figure 75)**.

2. Select any file with a Status listed as Missing **(Figure 76)**.

3. *Optional:* Click Show Me to see the picture selected in the active document.

4. Click Update to search for the missing picture file.

5. Select the correct picture file in the "Find..." dialog box.

6. Click Open **(Figure 77)**.

Figure 75. *Select **Picture Usage** from the **Utilities** menu.*

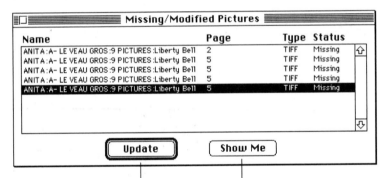

Figure 76. *Click **Update** to search for a missing picture file.*

*Click **Show Me** to see a picture selected in the document.*

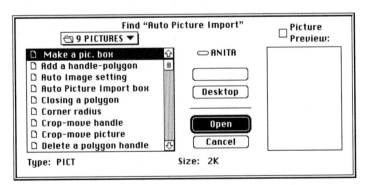

Figure 77. *Select a picture file, then click **Open** to update it.*

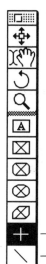

Figure 1. *The Line tools in the Tool palette.*

*The **Orthogonal Line tool** draws only vertical and horizontal lines.*

*The **Line tool** draws lines at any angle.*

About Lines:

The line creation tools are used to create horizontal, vertical, and diagonal lines and arrows to which a variety of styles and endcaps can be applied. To place rules under type, use the Paragraph Rules feature. *(See Chapter 7, Paragraph Rules)*

To draw a line using the Orthogonal Line tool:

1. Select the Orthogonal Line tool **(Figure 1)**.

2. Press and drag the crosshair icon horizontally or vertically **(Figure 2)**.

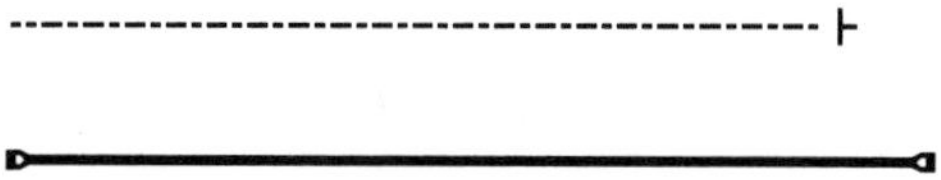

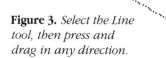

Figure 2. *Select the Orthogonal Line tool, then press and drag.*

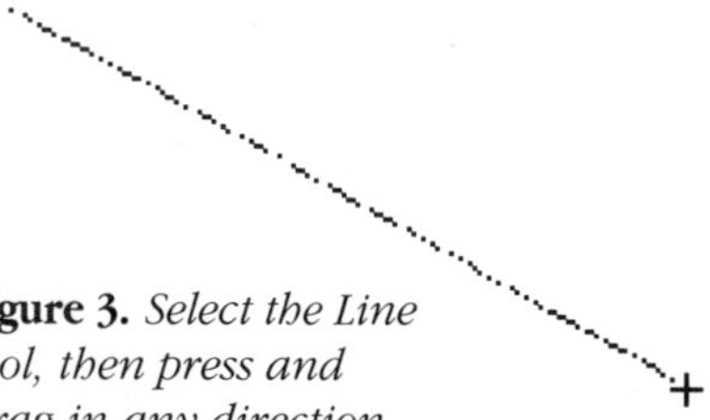

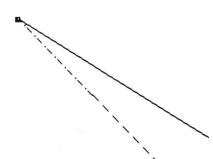

Figure 3. *Select the Line tool, then press and drag in any direction.*

To draw a line using the Line tool:

1. Select the Line tool **(Figure 1)**.

2. Press and drag the crosshair icon in any direction **(Figure 3)**.

✔ Tips

■ Hold down Shift while drawing a line to constrain the line to a 45° angle. An existing line can be reset to a 45° angle by dragging on a handle with Shift held down **(Figure 4)**.

■ To keep a Line tool selected, hold down Option and select it. Deselect it by selecting another tool.

Figure 4. *To snap a line to a 45° angle, drag a handle with Shift held down.*

Draw a Line

To style a line using the Measurements palette:

1. Select the Item or Content tool.

2. Select a line **(Figure 5)**.

3. In the Width field, enter a width between 0 and 504 points in increments as small as .001, then press Return **(Figures 6-7)**.

and/or

Select from the eleven line styles in the Style pop-up menu.

and/or

Select from the six endcap styles in the Endcap pop-up menu.

✔ Tip

■ A line can also be styled using the Line Style, Endcaps, Width, Color or Shade pop-up menu under the Style menu, or using the Line Specifications dialog box, opened by selecting Modify from the Item menu.
(See Chapter 9, Apply Color)

To modify the width of a line using the keyboard:

1. Select the Item or Content tool.

2. Select a line.

3. Hold down Command (⌘), Option, Shift and press the > key to enlarge or the < key to reduce the width of the line in 1 point increments.

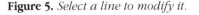

Figure 5. *Select a line to modify it.*

The width is increased to 6 points.

A new style is applied.

A new endcap is applied.

*The line **Style** pop-up menu.*

*The line **Width** field.*

	X1 : 3p11.453	X2 : 7p.541	Endpoints	W : 2 pt
	Y1 : 2p2.465	Y2 : 2p2.465		

Figure 6. *The Measurements palette with a line selected.*

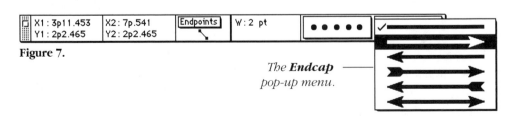

	X1 : 3p11.453	X2 : 7p.541	Endpoints	W : 2 pt
	Y1 : 2p2.465	Y2 : 2p2.465		

Figure 7.

*The **Endcap** pop-up menu.*

Figure 8. *Press and drag an endpoint to resize a line.*

Figure 9. *Non-printing lines can create interesting text shapes. Select a line and then check the Suppress Printout box in the Line Specifications dialog box opened by selecting Modify from the Item menu.*

To resize a line manually:

1. Select the Item or Content tool.

2. Select a line.

3. Press and drag an endpoint to lengthen or shorten the line **(Figure 8)**.

To resize a line using the Measurements palette:

1. Select the Item or Content tool.

2. Select a line.

3. Select Left Point, Midpoint or Right Point from the Mode pop-up menu in the Measurements palette. The line will be measured from the chosen point **(Figure 10)**.

4. Enter a number in the Length field next to the "L" **(Figure 11)**.

5. Press Return.

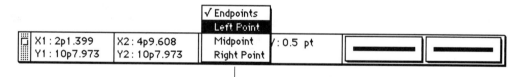

Figure 10. *Select **Left Point**, **Midpoint**, or **Right Point** mode from the Measurements palette.*

The angle of a line can be modified in the rotation angle field. This field is not available when Endpoints mode is selected.

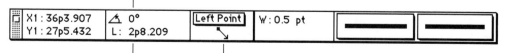

Figure 11. *The **Length** field.*

This icon illustrates the selected mode by indicating the beginning and ending points of the line.

Resize a Line

To move a line manually:

1. Select the Item or Content tool.

2. Press on any part of a line other than an endpoint and drag in any direction **(Figure 12)**.

✔ Tip

■ To maintain a line's original angle of rotation while it is moved, hold down Shift and press and drag. Release the mouse before releasing Shift.

To reposition a line using the Measurements palette:

1. Select the Item or Content tool.

2. Select a line.

3. Select a mode from the Mode pop-up menu in the Measurements palette **(Figure 10)**.

4. Enter numbers in the X and/or Y fields **(Figures 13-14)**.

5. Press Return.

Figure 12. *To move a line, press and drag it with the Item tool.*

*The **horizontal** position of the left point of a line.*

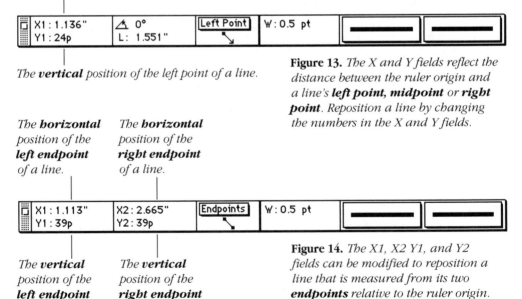

*The **vertical** position of the left point of a line.*

Figure 13. *The X and Y fields reflect the distance between the ruler origin and a line's **left point, midpoint** or **right point**. Reposition a line by changing the numbers in the X and Y fields.*

*The **horizontal** position of the **left endpoint** of a line.*

*The **horizontal** position of the **right endpoint** of a line.*

*The **vertical** position of the **left endpoint** of a line.*

*The **vertical** position of the **right endpoint** of a line.*

Figure 14. *The X1, X2 Y1, and Y2 fields can be modified to reposition a line that is measured from its two **endpoints** relative to the ruler origin.*

STYLE SHEETS 11

About style sheets:

A style sheet is a set of paragraph and character formatting specifications that can be applied to one or more selected paragraphs with a quick keystroke or by clicking in the Style Sheets palette. If a style sheet is modified, all paragraphs to which it has been applied will be reformatted automatically.

A document can contain up to 127 Style Sheets **(Figure 1)**.

THE BILL OF RIGHTS — *A Headline style.*

AMENDMENT I. — *A Subhead style.*
Religious establishment prohibited.
Freedom of speech, of the press, and right to petition.
Congress shall make no law respecting an establishment of religion, or prohibiting the free exercise thereof; or abridging the freedom of speech, or of the press; or the right of the people peaceably to assemble, and to petition the Government for a redress of grievances. — *A Body Text style.*

AMENDMENT II.
Right to keep and bear arms. — *A Small Subhead style.*
A well-regulated militia, being necessary to the security of a free State, the right of the people to keep and bear arms, shall not be infringed.

AMENDMENT III.
Conditions for quarters for soldiers.
No soldier shall, in time of peace be quartered in any house, without the consent of the owner, nor in time of war, but in a manner to be prescribed by law.

AMENDMENT IV.
Right of search and seizure regulated.
The right of the people to be secure in their persons, houses, papers, and effects, against unreasonable searches and seizures, shall not be violated, and no warrants shall issue, but upon probable cause, supported by oath or affirmation, and particularly describing the place to be searched, and the persons or things to be seized.

Figure 1. *Use style sheets to apply repeated paragraph specifications quickly.*

To create a new style sheet:

1. Format a paragraph using any of the character, paragraph, tab or rule options available under the Style menu. This will be referred to as a "sample" paragraph.

2. With the cursor in the "sample" paragraph, select Style Sheets from the Edit menu **(Figure 2)**.

3. Click New **(Figure 3)**.

4. Enter a name for the new style sheet in the Name field in the Edit Style Sheet dialog box **(Figure 4)**.

5. *Optional:* Press Tab to move the cursor to the Keyboard Equivalent field, and press any function key (other than F1-F4) or keypad key alone or in combination with one or more of the Command (⌘), Option, Shift, or Control keys.

6. Click OK or press Return.

7. Click Save **(Figure 5)**.

✔ Tips

■ The new style sheet should be applied to the "sample" paragraph in addition to any other paragraphs.

■ The style sheet can be edited later, if desired.
 (See Edit a Style Sheet in this chapter)

■ A new style sheet can also be created by selecting Style Sheets from the Edit menu without clicking in a "sample" paragraph. Click New in the Style Sheets dialog box, enter a name for the new style sheet, then follow steps 3-6 on page 130.

Edit

Undo Deletion	⌘Z
Cut	⌘H
Copy	⌘C
Paste	⌘U
Clear	
Select All	⌘A
Subscribe To...	
Subscriber Options...	
Show Clipboard	
Find/Change	⌘F
Preferences	▶
Style Sheets...	
Colors...	
H&Js...	

Figure 2. *With the cursor in a "sample" paragraph, select **Style Sheets** from the **Edit** menu.*

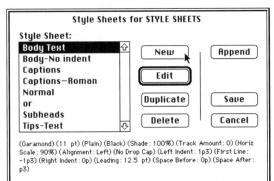

Figure 3. *Click **New** in the Style Sheets dialog box to create a new style sheet.*

Create a Style Sheet

*Enter a **Name** for the style sheet. (Assign a descriptive name, such as "Body Text," or "Headlines.")* ——

*Enter a **Keyboard Equivalent** for the style sheet.* ——

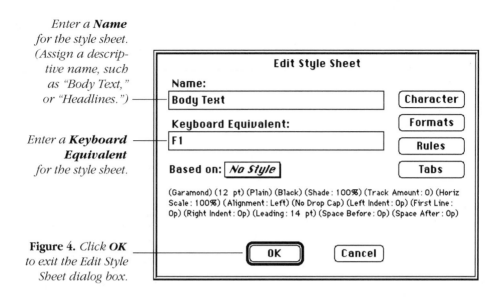

Figure 4. *Click **OK** to exit the Edit Style Sheet dialog box.*

*Style sheets are listed in the **Style Sheet** scroll list.* ——

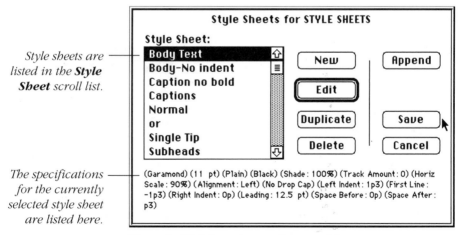

The specifications for the currently selected style sheet are listed here. ——

Figure 5. *Click **Save** to save the new style sheet and exit the Style Sheets dialog box.*

To apply a style sheet using the Style Sheets palette:

1. Display the Style Sheets palette by selecting Show Style Sheets from the View menu **(Figure 6)**.

2. Click in a paragraph or press and drag through a series of paragraphs.

3. Click on a style sheet name in the Style Sheets palette. The paragraph or paragraphs will be instantly reformatted **(Figure 7)**.

✔ Tips

■ Text that is formatted using a style sheet can still be locally formatted using the Measurements palette, keyboard, or Style menu.

■ To clear a style sheet and all local formatting from a paragraph and apply a new style sheet in one keystroke, hold down Option, then click on the name of the new style sheet in the Style Sheets palette.

■ Style sheets can also be applied using the Style Sheets pop-up menu opened from the Style menu.

To apply a style sheet using the keyboard:

1. Click in a paragraph or press and drag through a series of paragraphs.

2. Perform the keyboard equivalent assigned to the chosen style sheet.

✔ Tip

■ The keyboard equivalent for each style sheet is listed next to the style sheet name in the Style Sheets palette **(Figure 7)** and in the Style Sheets pop-up menu under the Style menu.

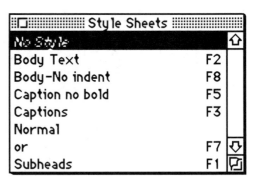

View

✓ Fit in Window   ⌘0
  50%
  75%
  Actual Size   ⌘1
  200%
  Thumbnails

  Hide Guides
  Show Baseline Grid
  Snap to Guides
  Hide Rulers   ⌘R
  Show Invisibles   ⌘I

  Hide Tools
  Hide Measurements
  Show Document Layout
  Show Style Sheets
  Show Colors
  Show Trap Information
  Show Value Converter
  Windows   ▶

Figure 6. *Select **Show Style Sheets** from the **View** menu.*

Style Sheets

No Style
Body Text   F2
Body–No indent   F8
Caption no bold   F5
Captions   F3
Normal
or   F7
Subheads   F1

Figure 7. *Click on any name in the Style Sheets palette to apply a style sheet.*

Apply a Style Sheet

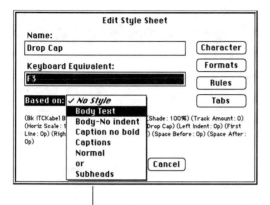

Figure 8. *To base one style sheet on another, select a style sheet from the **Based on** pop-up menu in the Edit Style Sheet dialog box.*

About Based On style sheets:

A new style sheet can be created based on an existing style sheet. The new style sheet is linked to the original style sheet on which it is based. If the original style sheet is modified, any style sheets that are based on it will also change.

For example, a "Drop Cap" style sheet can be created based on a "Body Text" style sheet, adding an automatic drop cap. Modifications made to the "Body Text" style sheet will automatically be made to the "Drop Cap" style sheet.

To base one style sheet on another style sheet:

1. Select Style Sheets from the Edit menu.
2. Click New.
3. Enter a name for the new style sheet **(Figure 9)**.
4. *Optional:* Enter a Keyboard Equivalent.
5. Select a style sheet from the Based on pop-up menu **(Figure 8)**.
6. Edit the style sheet by following steps 3 and 4 on the following page.
7. Click OK to exit the Edit Style Sheet dialog box.
8. Click Save.

Figure 9. *The Edit Style Sheet dialog box of a "Based On" style.*

*The name of the style sheet that the current style sheet is **Based on** is displayed here.*

The specifications listed in the Edit Style Sheet dialog box indicate that this "Drop Cap" style is based on the "Body Text" style, with the Drop Cap option added.

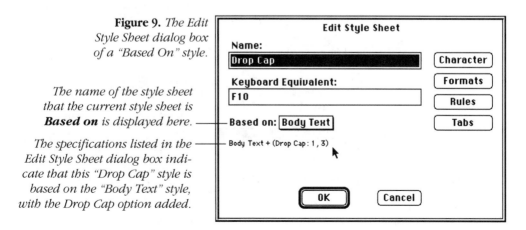

To edit a style sheet:

1. Select Style Sheets from the Edit
menu and select a style sheet name
(Figure 10).

> *or*

> If the Style Sheets palette is open,
> click in a text box to activate it, hold
> down Command (⌘), and click on a
> style sheet name in the palette.

2. Click Edit **(Figure 11)**.

3. Click Character, Formats, Rules or Tabs
to open the corresponding dialog box
or boxes. Modify text attributes in the
Character dialog box; modify paragraph
formatting in the Paragraph Formats
dialog box; add, delete or edit a rule in
the Paragraph Rules dialog box; or add,
delete or modify tabs in the Paragraph
Tabs dialog box **(Figure 12)**.

4. Click OK or press Return to exit the
Character, Formats, Rules, or Tabs
dialog box.

5. Click OK to exit the Edit Style Sheet
dialog box.

6. Click Save to exit the Style Sheets
dialog box. Paragraphs to which the
style sheet has already been applied
will be instantly reformatted.

Figure 10. *Hold down* **Command** *(⌘)
and click on a style sheet name to open
the Style Sheets dialog box.*

Edit a Style Sheet

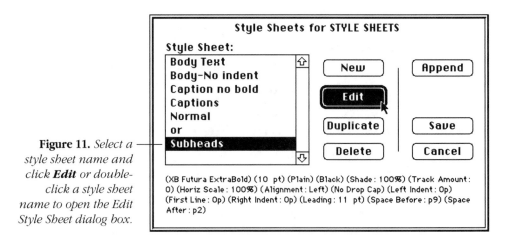

Figure 11. *Select a
style sheet name and
click* **Edit** *or double-
click a style sheet
name to open the Edit
Style Sheet dialog box.*

*The **Name** and **Keyboard Equivalent***
for a style sheet can be changed here.

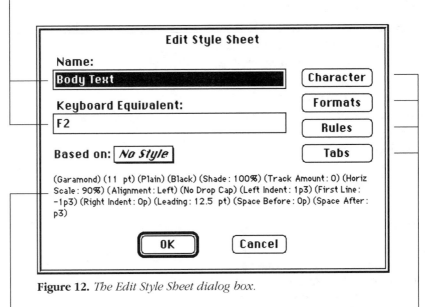

Figure 12. *The Edit Style Sheet dialog box.*

The current specifications for
the style sheet are listed here.

*Click **Character, Formats,***
***Rules** or **Tabs** to open*
the corresponding dialog
box or boxes.

About Default Style Sheets.

The Normal style sheet is the default style sheet for all newly created text boxes. If the Normal style sheet is modified with a file open, text entered in any newly created text boxes or text to which the Normal style sheet is already applied will be affected within the active file only. If the Normal style sheet is modified with no file open, the Normal style sheet will be modified for all subsequently created files. Any style sheet created with no file open will be added to the Style Sheets palette of all subsequently created files.

To append style sheets from one file to another:

1. Select Style Sheets from the Edit menu.

2. Click Append **(Figure 13)**.

3. Select the file containing the style sheet or sheets to be appended **(Figure 14)**.

4. Click Open. The appended style sheets will be listed in the Style Sheet scroll list **(Figure 15)**.

5. For each appended style sheet that you **don't** want to save, select it and click Delete.

6. Click Save to exit the Style Sheets dialog box.

✔ Tips

■ If a style sheet that you are attempting to append has the **same name** as a style sheet in the active file you are appending to, the style sheet will not be appended.

■ If a style sheet that you are attempting to append has the **same keyboard equivalent** as a style sheet in the active file you are appending to, the style sheet will be appended, but the keyboard equivalent will not be appended.

■ If text with a style sheet or sheets applied to it is pasted from another document using the Clipboard, drag-copied from another document, or retrieved from a library, the style sheet or sheets will be appended, with the above-mentioned name conflict being the only exception.

■ Style sheets can be appended from a document created in Microsoft Word 3.0 or later. The Microsoft Word filter must be in the QuarkXPress folder when the application is launched.

Figure 13. *Click **Append** in the Style Sheets dialog box.*

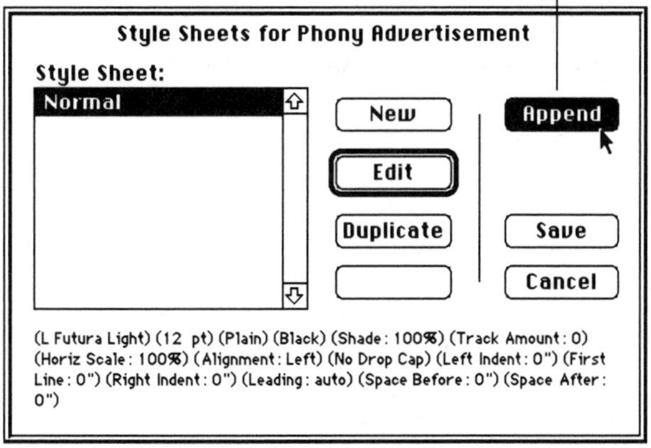

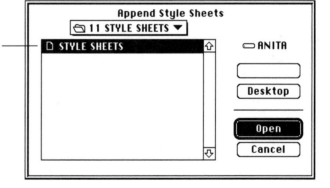

Figure 14. *Select the file to be appended from in the Append Style Sheets dialog box, then click **Open**.*

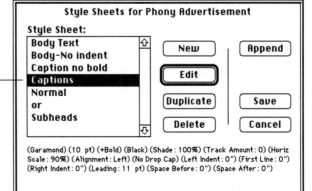

Figure 15. *The appended style sheets are now listed in the **Style Sheet** scroll list. Select and delete any style sheets you don't want to save, then click **Save**.*

About the Duplicate option:

The Duplicate command is used to create a copy of an existing style sheet. There is no linkage between a Duplicate style sheet and the original from which it is generated.

To duplicate a style sheet:

1. Select Style Sheets from the Edit menu **(Figure 16)**.

2. Select a style sheet name.

3. Click Duplicate **(Figure 17)**.

4. The Edit Style Sheet dialog box will automatically open, and the name of the style sheet will appear in the Name field, prefaced by "Copy of." Edit the name, if desired **(Figure 18)**.

5. Edit the new style sheet, if desired.

6. Click OK.

7. Click Save.

To delete a style sheet:

1. Select Style Sheets from the Edit menu.

2. Select a style sheet name.

3. Click Delete **(Figure 17)**.

4. When the prompt appears, click OK. Where the style sheet has been applied, it will be replaced with No Style.

5. Click Save.

✔ Tip

■ The Normal style sheet can be edited, but it cannot deleted.

Figure 16. *Select **Style Sheets** from the **Edit** menu.*

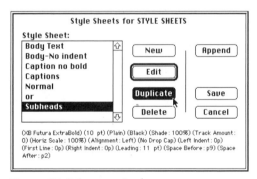

Figure 17. *Select a style sheet name, then click **Duplicate**.*

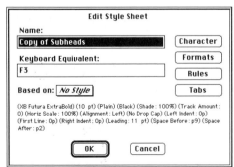

Figure 18. *The new style sheet name will be prefaced by "Copy of." A new name can be assigned.*

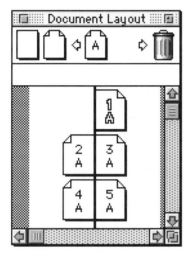

Figure 1. *The Document Layout palette of a facing-page document.*

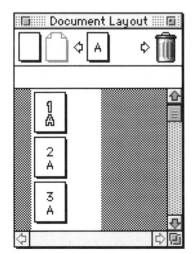

Figure 2. *The Document Layout palette of a single-sided document.*

About master pages:

A master page is a special formatting page containing elements that repeat on each document page to which it is applied. Master pages expedite the production of documents like newsletters, magazines and books where the same headers, footers, lines, etc. recur on many pages.

Master pages are created, edited, and applied using the Document Layout palette. When a master page icon is dragged over a document page icon on the palette, the document page automatically takes on the guides, items and page-numbering from the master page. The master elements can be locally edited on the document page. All new documents contain a Master A page. Up to 126 additional master pages can be created.

(See Chapter 1, The Document Layout palette)

About single-sided and facing-page documents:

When the Facing Pages box is checked in the New dialog box, page 1 will be alone on the right-hand side, and the remaining pages arranged side-by-side in pairs, with even-numbered pages on the left and odd-numbered pages on the right. The facing-page format is used for book layouts. In the Document Layout palette of a facing-page document, master and document page icons have turned-down corners **(Figure 1)**.

When the Facing Pages box is unchecked in the New dialog box, pages are single-sided. In the Document Layout palette of a single-sided document, master and document page icons have square corners **(Figure 2)**. Multi-page spreads can be created by moving page icons side-by side.

(See Chapter 6, Figures 14a-b)

To number pages automatically:

1. Select Show Document Layout from the View menu **(Figure 3)**.

2. Display the Master A page by double-clicking the icon marked "A" on the top row of the Document Layout palette **(Figure 4)**.

3. Select the Text Box tool.

4. Press and drag to create a small text box for the page number.

5. Hold down Command (⌘) and press "3". Any prefix, such as "Page," can be entered before the page numbering command. Enter the command on both the left and right master pages if you are working on a facing-page document **(Figure 5)**.

6. Return to the document by double-clicking a page icon in the Document Layout palette.

✔ Tips

- If pages are added to or deleted from a document, the page numbers will be updated automatically.

- The Current Page Number command can be entered on a document page, but only that page will be numbered.

Figure 3. *Select **Show Document Layout** from the View menu.*

View	
Fit in Window	⌘0
50%	
75%	
Actual Size	⌘1
200%	
Thumbnails	
Hide Guides	
Show Baseline Grid	
Snap to Guides	
Hide Rulers	⌘R
Show Invisibles	⌘I
Hide Tools	
Hide Measurements	
Show Document Layout	
Show Style Sheets	
Show Colors	
Show Trap Information	
Show Value Converter	
Windows	▶

Items such as a header, picture box, or vertical rule can be placed on a master page.

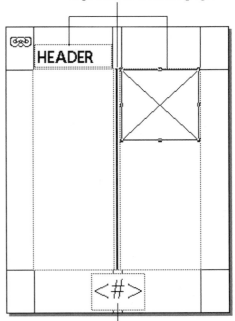

Figure 5. *The **Current Page Number** command displays as "<#>".*

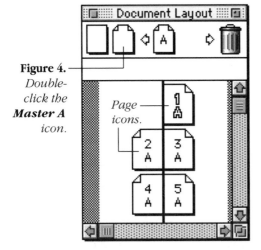

Figure 4. *Double-click the **Master A** icon.*

Page icons.

Automatic Page Numbering

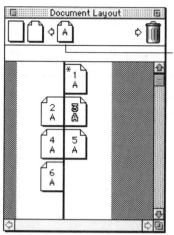

Figure 6.
Double-click a lettered master page icon.

Note: Select Show Document Layout from the View menu to open the Document Layout palette for the following procedures **(Figure 3)**.

To modify a master page:

1. Double-click a master page icon on the top row of the Document Layout palette **(Figure 6)**.

2. Add any new master items, such as a header, footer, line, or picture.
or
Modify any existing master items.

✔ Tips

■ Pages to which the master has already been applied will be modified. Previous master items that were locally modified in the document will not be affected by new modifications on the master page. *(See Apply a Master Page in this chapter)*

■ Text should not be entered in the automatic text box on a master page, but can be entered in any other box.

■ In a facing-page document, each master page has a left and right page. Items placed on a left facing master page will appear only on left (even-numbered) document pages.

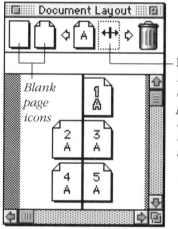

Figure 7a.
Press and drag a blank page icon to a position between the arrows.

Blank page icons

To create a new master page:

Press and drag a blank single-sided or facing-page icon to a position between the arrows on the top row of the Document Layout palette. The new master page will be labeled with the next letter of the alphabet **(Figures 7a-7b)**.

To rename a master page:

Click once on a master page icon, and enter up to 64 characters in the name field below the master page icons. The letters on the master page icons themselves cannot be changed **(Figure 7b)**.

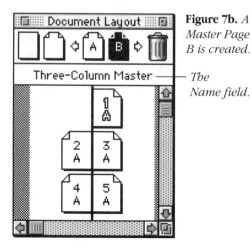

Figure 7b. *A Master Page B is created.*

— The Name field.

Three-Column Master

Modify, Create, or Rename a Master Page

To apply a master page to a document page:

1. Press and drag a master page icon over a document page icon in the Document Layout palette. Release the mouse when the document page icon is highlighted **(Figures 8a-8b)**.

2. Return to the document by double-clicking a page icon in the Document Layout palette.

✔ Tips

■ If Delete Changes is selected from the Master Page Items pop-up menu in the General Preferences dialog box, opened from the Edit menu, and a master page is applied or reapplied to a document page, locally modified and unmodified master items will be deleted from the document page. If Keep Changes is selected from the same pop-up menu, only unmodified master items will be deleted.

■ The Display pop-up menu under the Page menu can also be used to display master pages and document pages. If Document is selected when a master page is currently displayed, the last displayed document page will be displayed again.

■ If a page or pages are drag-copied from one file to another, any applied master pages will also be appended. *(See first Tip on page 58)*

■ If an odd number of pages is added to or deleted from a facing-page document and document pages are reshuffled, the corresponding left and right master pages are automatically applied to the reshuffled pages.

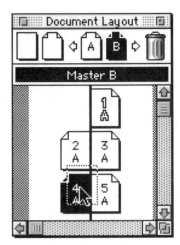

Figure 8a. *Press and drag a master page icon over a document page icon.*

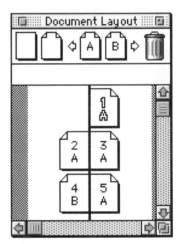

Figure 8b. *All of the items on Master Page B have been added to document page 4.*

Apply a Master Page

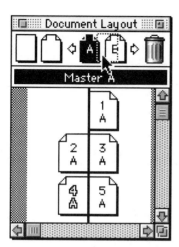

Figure 9. *Drag one master page icon over another to copy master items. In this illustration, all the Master Page A items are being copied onto Master Page B.*

Note: Select Show Document Layout from the View menu to open the Document Layout palette for the following procedures **(Figure 3)**.

To replace the items on one master page with items from another master page:

1. Press and drag a master page icon onto another master page icon in the Document Layout palette **(Figure 9)**.

2. Click OK or press Return when the warning prompt appears.

To modify the non-printing margin and column guides:

1. Double-click a master page icon in the Document Layout Palette.

2. Select Master Guides from the Page menu **(Figure 10)**.

3. Modify the numbers in the Margin Guides fields **(Figure 11)**.
and/or
Modify the numbers in the Column Guides fields.

4. Click OK or press Return.

✔ Tip

■ If a master page's guides are modified, all pages to which that master page has been applied will display the new guides. Any automatic text box that fits within the margin guides will resize to fit into the new margin guides, and will also reflect the number of columns specified.

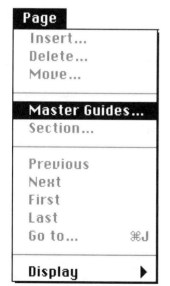

Figure 10. *Select **Master Guides** from the **Page** menu.*

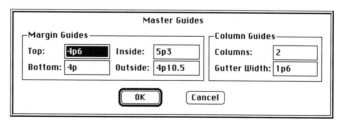

Figure 11. *The non-printing **Margin Guides** and **Column Guides** are modified in the Master Guides dialog box.*

About numbering sections:

Documents containing more than one section may require more than one page numbering format. For example, in this book, the lowercase Roman format is used for the Table of Contents and the numeric format is used for the pages that follow. A document that is divided into more than one file may also require special starting page numbers.

To number a section of a file:

1. To display the page where the new section is to begin, select Go to from the Page menu.

2. Enter the number of the page that is to begin the new section.

3. Click OK or press Return.

4. Select Section from the Page menu **(Figure 12)**.

5. Check the Section Start box **(Figure 13)**.

Steps 6-8 are optional.

6. Modify the default starting Number.

7. Enter a maximum of four characters in the Prefix field.

8. Select an alternate numbering Format.

9. Click OK or press Return.

✔ Tip

■ The number of the first page in a section will be marked with an asterisk in the current page number field and on the corresponding page icon in the Document Layout palette.
(See also the second Tip on page 32)

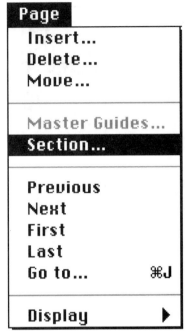

Figure 12. Select **Section** *from the* **Page** *menu.*

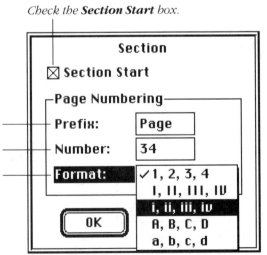

Check the **Section Start** *box.*

Enter a **Prefix**.

Leave the default **Number** *at 1 or enter a new number.*

Select one of the five numbering **Formats**.

Figure 13. *The Section dialog box.*

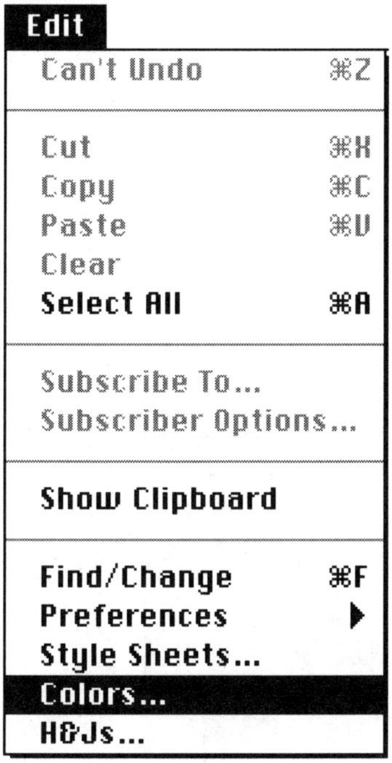

Figure 1. *Select **Colors** from the **Edit** menu.*

About color:

Two basic methods are used for printing color: spot color and process color.

A separate plate is used to print each **spot color**. Spot color inks are mixed according to specifications defined in a color matching system, such as Pantone.

Four plates are used to print **process color**, one each for cyan (C), magenta (M), yellow (Y) and black (K). A layer of tiny colored dots is printed from each plate; the overlapping dots create an illusion of color.

Computer monitors display additive color by projecting light and printers produce subtractive color using ink. Because computer monitors do not accurately display ink equivalents, colors should be specified using formulas defined in process and spot color guides, and not mixed based on screen representations.

Spot and process colors can be combined in the same color palette in QuarkXPress. Up to 127 colors can be created per file.

To create a spot color:

1. Select Colors from the Edit menu **(Figure 1)**.

2. Click New **(Figure 2)**.

3. Select Pantone from the Model pop-up menu **(Figure 3)**.

4. Enter a number from a Pantone color guide in the Pantone No. field.
   or
   Select a color in the "swatch" window.

5. Make sure the Process Separation check box is **unchecked.**

6. Click OK or press Return.

7. Click Save **(Figure 4)**.

(Continued on the following page)

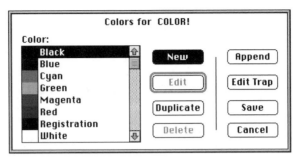

Figure 2. *Click* ***New*** *to create a new color.*

Figure 3. *Select* ***Pantone*** *from the* ***Model*** *pop-up menu in the Edit Color dialog box.*

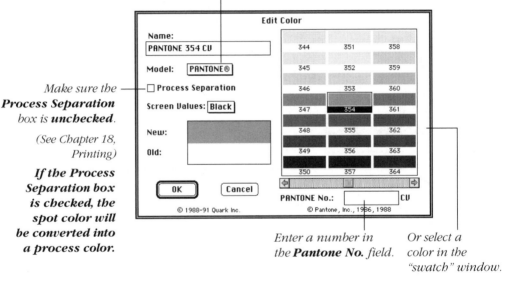

Make sure the **Process Separation** *box is* **unchecked**.

(See Chapter 18, Printing)

If the Process Separation box is checked, the spot color will be converted into a process color.

Enter a number in the ***Pantone No.*** *field.*

Or select a color in the "swatch" window.

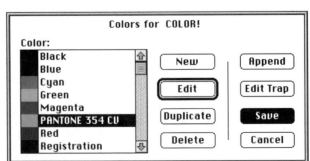

Figure 4. *The new Pantone color is now listed in the Colors dialog box, and is added to the Colors palette. Click* ***Save*** *to Exit.*

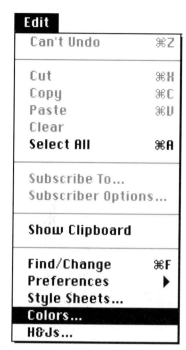

Edit

Can't Undo	⌘Z
Cut	⌘X
Copy	⌘C
Paste	⌘V
Clear	
Select All	⌘A
Subscribe To...	
Subscriber Options...	
Show Clipboard	
Find/Change	⌘F
Preferences	▶
Style Sheets...	
Colors...	
H&Js...	

Figure 5. *Select **Colors** from the **Edit** menu.*

To create a process color:

1. Select Colors from the Edit menu **(Figure 5)**.

2. Click New **(Figure 2)**.

3. Select CMYK from the Model pop-up menu, enter percentages in the Cyan, Magenta, Yellow, and Black fields, and then enter a name for the new color in the Name field **(Figure 6)**.
or
Select Trumatch or Focoltone from the Model pop-up menu, and select a color in the "swatch" window.

4. Make sure the Process Separation box is **checked**.

5. Click OK or press Return.

6. Click Save. The color will be added to the colors palette.

✔ Tips

■ If a color is created with no file open, it will be added to the default palette of subsequently created documents.

■ The RGB Model should be used if the file is to be output to a film recorder or created solely for display on a monitor.

Figure 6. *Enter a **Name** for a new CMYK color in the Edit Color dialog box.*

*Select CMYK, Trumatch, or Focoltone from the **Model** pop-up menu.*

*Make sure the **Process Separation** box is **checked**.*

*If the **Process Separation** box is unchecked, the process color will be converted into a spot color.*

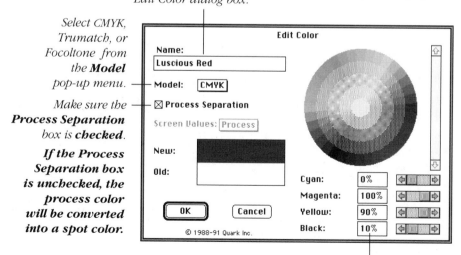

Edit Color

Name:
`Luscious Red`

Model: `CMYK`

☒ Process Separation

Screen Values: `Process`

New:

Old:

[**OK**]   [Cancel]

© 1988-91 Quark Inc.

Cyan:	0%	◀ ▮ ▶
Magenta:	100%	◀ ▮ ▶
Yellow:	90%	◀ ▮ ▶
Black:	10%	◀ ▮ ▶

*Enter percentages for **Cyan, Magenta, Yellow,** and **Black**.*

To edit a process color:

1. Select Colors from the Edit menu.

or

Hold down Command (⌘) and click a color in the Colors palette.

2. Select a color in the Colors dialog box and click Edit **(Figure 7)**.

or

Double-click a color.

*To append a color or colors from another QuarkXPress file, click **Append**. A color with the same name as a color in the active file will not be appended.*

3. Modify any of the Cyan, Magenta, Yellow or Black percentages **(Figure 8)**.

4. Click OK.

5. Click Save.

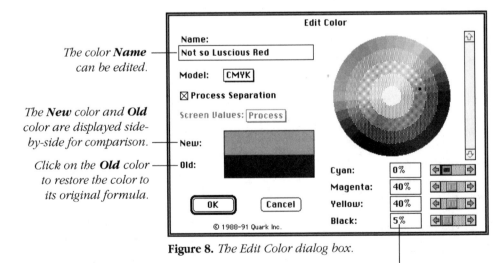

Figure 7. *Select a color, then click **Edit**.*

*Click **Delete** to remove selected color from the color palette. Cyan, Magenta, Yellow, Black, White and Registration cannot be deleted.*

*The color **Name** can be edited.*

*The **New** color and **Old** color are displayed side-by-side for comparison.*

*Click on the **Old** color to restore the color to its original formula.*

Figure 8. *The Edit Color dialog box.*

*Modify any of the **Cyan, Magenta, Yellow,** or **Black** percentages.*

Edit a Color

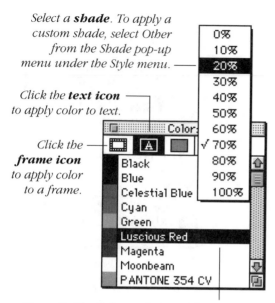

Select a **shade***. To apply a custom shade, select Other from the Shade pop-up menu under the Style menu.* ——

Click the **text icon** *to apply color to text.*

Click the **frame icon** *to apply color to a frame.*

Select a **color***.*

Figure 9. *The Colors palette when a* **text box** *is selected.*

To apply color to text:

1. Select Show Colors from the View menu to display the Colors palette **(Figure 15)**.

2. Select the Content tool.

3. Highlight the text to which color is to be applied.

4. Click the text icon in the Colors palette **(Figure 9)**.

5. Select a color.

6. Select a shade from the Shade pop-up menu **(Figures 10-11)**.

✔ Tip

■ A color or shade can also be applied to text using the Color or Shade pop-up menu under the Style menu, or using the Character dialog box, opened from the Style menu.

TWENTYPERCENT

THIRTYPERCENT

FORTY PERCENT

FIFTY PERCENT

SIXTY PERCENT

SEVENTYPERCENT

EIGHTYPERCENT

NINETYPERCENT

HUNDREDPERCENT

Figure 10. *A range of shades can be applied to type.*

CREATIVE MINDS

ALWAYS HAVE BEEN KNOWN TO SURVIVE ANY

KIND OF BAD TRAINING.

Anna Freud

Figure 11. *"Reversed" type.*

To apply color to a frame:

1. Select Show Colors from the View menu to display the Colors palette **(Figure 15)**.

2. Select the Item or Content tool.

3. Click on a text or picture box.

4. Click the frame icon in the Colors palette **(Figure 9)**.

5. Select a color.

6. Select a shade from the Shade pop-up menu.

✔ Tip

■ The frame width must be specified in the Frame dialog box, opened from the Item menu.

Apply Color

To apply color to a picture:

1. Select Show Colors from the View menu to display the Colors palette **(Figure 15)**.

2. Select the Content tool.

3. Click on a black-and-white bitmap, or TIFF or RIFF line art or grayscale picture.

4. Click the picture icon in the Colors palette **(Figure 12)**.

5. Select a color.

6. *Optional:* Select a shade percentage from the Shade pop-up menu for a black-and-white bitmap or TIFF or RIFF line art picture.

✔ Tips

■ A color can also be applied to a picture using the Color pop-up menu under the Style menu.

■ To color separate a TIFF picture from QuarkXPress, convert it to CMYK mode in another application before importing it.

Click the
picture icon.   *Select a* **shade**.

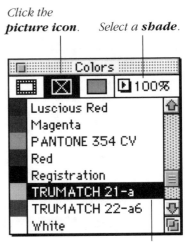

Select a **color**.

Figure 12. *The Colors palette when a* **picture box** *is selected.*

To apply color to a line:

1. Select Show Colors from the View menu to display the Colors palette **(Figure 15)**.

2. Select the Item or Content tool.

3. Select a line.

4. Click the line icon in the Colors palette **(Figure 13)**.

5. Select a color.

6. Select a shade percentage from the Shade pop-up menu.

✔ Tip

■ A color can also be applied to a line using the Color pop-up menu under the Style menu.

Click the
line icon.   *Select a* **shade**.

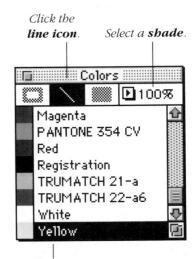

Select a **color**.

Figure 13. *The Colors palette when a* **line** *is selected.*

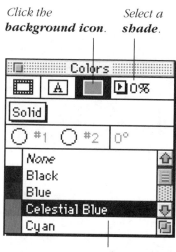

Click the **background icon**. *Select a* **shade**.

Select a **color**.

Figure 14. *The background icon is available on the Colors palette when a* **text box** *or* **picture box** *is selected.*

View

Fit in Window	⌘0
50%	
75%	
Actual Size	⌘1
200%	
Thumbnails	
Hide Guides	
Show Baseline Grid	
Snap to Guides	
Hide Rulers	⌘R
Show Invisibles	⌘I
Hide Tools	
Hide Measurements	
Show Document Layout	
Show Style Sheets	
Show Colors	
Show Trap Information	
Show Value Converter	
Windows	▶

Figure 15. *Select* **Show Colors** *from the* **View** *menu.*

To apply color to the background of a box:

1. Select Show Colors from the View menu to display the Colors palette **(Figure 15)**.

2. Select the Item or Content tool.

3. Click on a text or picture box.

4. Click the background icon in the Colors palette **(Figure 14)**.

5. Select a color.

6. Select a shade percentage from the Shade pop-up menu.

✔ Tip

■ When coloring type white, or returning "reversed type" to black-on-white, change the type color before changing the background color, so the text will be easy to highlight.

About linear blends:

Two-color linear blends can be created in QuarkXPress 3.1. A blend can be applied to the background of a text box or picture box, but not to text, lines or frames.

To create a linear blend:

1. Select the Item tool.

2. Click a text or picture box.

3. Select Show Colors from the View menu to open the Colors palette **(Figure 15)**.

(Continued on the following page)

Apply Color; Create a Linear Blend

4. Click the Background icon **(Figure 18)**.

5. Select Linear Blend from the Fill-type pop-up menu.

6. Click the button for the #1 color, select a color, and select a percentage from the Shade pop-up menu.

7. Click the button for the #2 color, select a color, and select a percentage from the Shade pop-up menu **(Figure 19)**.

8. *Optional:* Enter an angle between -360° and 360° in increments as small as .001° in the Angle field **(Figures 16-17)**.

✔ Tip

■ A linear blend will be displayed in a deselected box, or in a selected box when the Item tool is selected. A linear blend will not be displayed in a selected box if the Content tool is selected.

Figure 16. *A black & white linear blend at a 90° angle.*

Figure 17. *A black & white linear blend at a 125° angle.*

Figure 18. *Select* **Linear Blend** *from the Fill-type pop-up menu.*

Click the **background icon***.*

Select a **shade***.*

The **angle** *of the blend can be modified.*

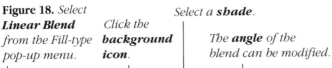

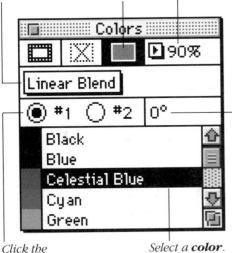

Click the **#1 color** *button.*

Select a **color***.*

Figure 19. *Click the* **#2 color** *button, then select a* **color** *and* **shade***.*

LIBRARIES 14

Utilities

Check Spelling ▶
Auxiliary Dictionary...

Suggested Hyphenation...　⌘H
Hyphenation Exceptions...

Library...

Font Usage...
Picture Usage...

Tracking Edit...
Kerning Table Edit...
Remove Manual Kerning
Alternate Em Spaces

Figure 1. *Select **Library** from the **Utilities** menu.*

About the Library feature:

Libraries are special files that store items that can be drag-copied onto any QuarkXPress page. Each library is displayed as a floating palette and can contain up to 2,000 entries. Up to seven libraries and/or documents can be open at a time, and an unlimited number can be created.

To create a library:

1. Select Library from the Utilities menu **(Figure 1)**.
2. Click New **(Figure 2)**.
3. Enter a name for the library in the New Library entry field **(Figure 3)**.
4. Select a drive or folder in which to save the library.
5. Click Create. A new library palette will be displayed.

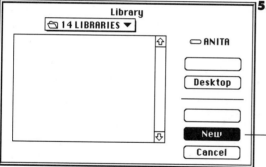

Figure 2. *Click **New**.*

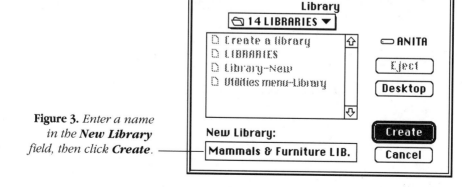

Figure 3. *Enter a name in the **New Library** field, then click **Create**.*

To open a library from within QuarkXPress:

1. Select Library from the Utilities menu **(Figure 4)**.

2. Select a library file.

3. Click Open **(Figure 5)**.

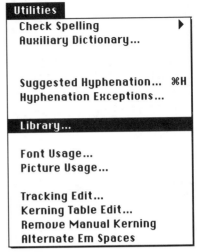

Figure 4. *Select **Library** from the **Utilities** menu.*

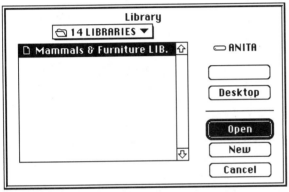

Figure 5. *Select a library file, then click **Open**.*

To open a library from the Desktop:

Double-click a library icon **(Figure 6).**

Figure 6. *Double-click a library icon from the Finder desktop.*

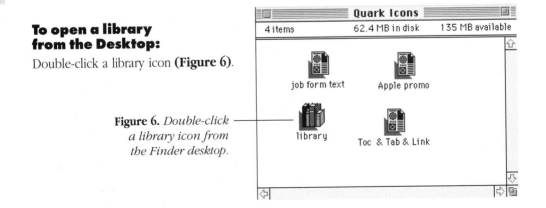

To add an entry to a library:

1. Open a library.
(Follow instructions on the previous page)

2. Select the Item tool.

3. Press and drag any item or group onto the Library palette **(Figures 7-9)**.

✔ Tip

■ A library is saved when an item is added to or deleted from it if the Auto Library Save box is checked in the Application Preferences dialog box, opened from the Edit menu. Otherwise, a library is saved only when it is closed.

To delete an entry from a library:

1. Select the Item or Content tool.

2. Select a library item.

3. Select Delete from the Item menu.
or
Hold down Command (⌘) and press "K".

Figure 7. *Press and drag an item into a library with the **Item** tool selected.*

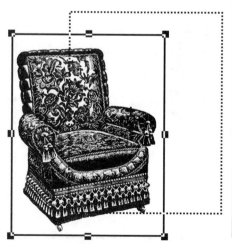

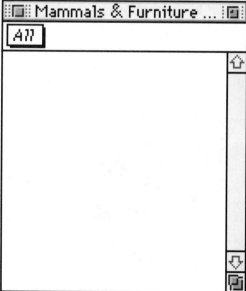

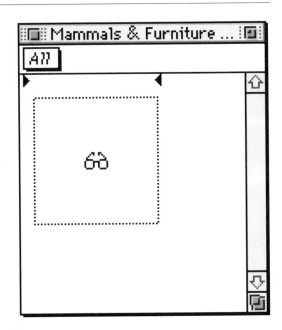

Figure 8. *The cursor turns into an eyeglasses icon as an entry is dragged into a library.*

Click the Close box to close a library palette.

Figure 9. *The entry is automatically duplicated, and the original is left intact. Entries can be rearranged within a library by pressing and dragging them.*

To retrieve an entry from a library:

1. Select the Item or Content tool.

2. Press and drag an item from a library onto a document page **(Figure 10)**.

✔ Tips

■ When an item with a color applied to it is retrieved from a library, the color is appended to the color palette of the active file.

■ When text with a style sheet applied to it is retrieved from a library, the style sheet is appended to the active file.

■ When a picture is added to a library, the path to the original picture file is stored with the library entry. When a picture is retrieved from a library, the picture's path is also stored with the document. The original picture file must be retained to print properly. *(See also Chapter 9, Import a Picture and Picture Usage)*

Click the Zoom box to display the library entries in horizontal rows.

Figure 10. *Press and drag an entry onto a document page.*

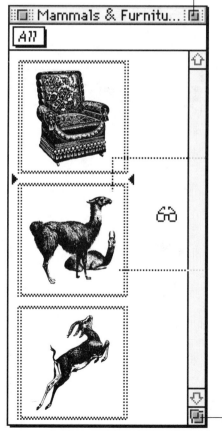

Press and drag the resize box to resize the palette.

Retrieve a Library Entry

About labeling library entries:

Labeling related library entries helps orga-
nize them. The same label can be applied
to numerous entries so that when a label is
selected from the Label pop-up menu, all
entries with that label are displayed. The
Label pop-up menu always displays "All"
and "Unlabeled." When a new label is created, it is added to the Label pop-up menu.

To label a library entry:

1. Double-click a library entry.

2. Enter a name in the Label field
(Figure 11).
or
Select an existing label from the Label
pop-up menu.

3. Click OK or press Return.

✔ Tip

■ The same label can be re-entered
for different entries, but it is easier to
select an existing label.

To display entries with the same label:

Select a label from the pop-up menu in
the library palette. Any number of labels
can be displayed at a time **(Figure 12)**.

Select All from the pop-up menu to display
all the entries in a library.

To hide entries with the same label:

Re-select a selected label from the pop-up
menu in the library palette. A selected label
has a check mark next to it **(Figure 12)**.

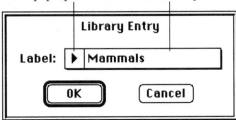

Figure 11. *Double-click a library entry and select an existing label from the* **Label** *pop-up menu.*   *Or enter a new label in the* **Label** *field.*

Figure 12. *A check mark indicates that entries with that label are currently displayed.*

Label a Library Entry

MULTIPLE ITEMS

Figure 1a. *Drag a marquee over multiple items with the Item tool.*

Victorian decorative initial

Victorian decorative initial

Figure 1b. *The handles indicate that both items are selected.*

Item	
Modify...	⌘M
Frame...	⌘B
Runaround...	⌘T
Duplicate	**⌘D**
Step and Repeat...	
Delete	**⌘K**
Group	**⌘G**
Ungroup	⌘U
Constrain	
Unlock	**⌘L**
Send to Back	
Bring to Front	
Space/Align...	
Picture Box Shape	▶
Reshape Polygon	

Figure 2. *Select **Group** from the **Item** menu.*

About the Group command:

Items that are grouped using the Group command remain associated as a unit until the Ungroup command is selected. For example, a picture and caption can be grouped so that they can be moved as a unit. Individual items within a group can be modified.

To group items:

1. Select the Item tool.

2. Hold down Shift and click once on each item to be included in the group. (To deselect an item from a multiple-selection and keep the remaining items selected, hold down Shift and click on the item.)

or

Position the cursor outside all the items to be included in the group, then press and drag a marquee around them. It is only necessary to drag over a portion of all the items (**Figures 1a and 1b**).

3. Select Group from the Item menu (**Figures 2-3**).

or

Hold down Command (⌘) and press "G".

Victorian decorative initial

Figure 3. *A dotted border surrounds a group that is selected with the Item tool.*

To move an item within a group:

1. Select the Content tool.

2. Hold down Command (⌘), press on an item to be moved, pause briefly for the item to redraw, then drag the item **(Figure 4)**.

Figure 4. *Select the Content tool, hold down Command (⌘) and press and drag an item. Note the Item tool icon.*

Victorian decorative initial

To delete an item from a group:

1. Select the Content tool.

2. Select an item to be deleted.

3. Select Delete from the Item menu.
or
Hold down Command (⌘) and press "K".

4. After the warning prompt appears, click OK or press Return **(Figure 5)**.

> ⚠ This will delete an item from a group and cannot be undone. OK to continue?
>
> [OK]
> [Cancel]

Figure 5. *This prompt will appear if you attempt to delete an item from a group.*

To ungroup items:

1. Select the Item tool.

2. Select a group.

3. Select Ungroup from the Item menu **(Figure 6)**.
or
Hold down Command (⌘) and press "U".

✔ Tips

■ Select the Content tool to modify the size or contents of an item in a group.

■ Groups can be multiple-selected and grouped into larger groups.

■ The background color and shade, angle of rotation, and position of a group can be modified by selecting the group with the Item tool, selecting Modify from the Item menu, and modifying any of the Group Specifications. Runaround options must be selected individually for each item in a group.

Item	
Modify...	⌘M
Frame...	⌘B
Runaround...	⌘T
Duplicate	⌘D
Step and Repeat...	
Delete	⌘K
Group	⌘G
Ungroup	**⌘U**
Constrain	
Lock	⌘L
Send to Back	
Bring to Front	
Space/Align...	
Picture Box Shape	▶
Reshape Polygon	

Figure 6. *Select **Ungroup** from the **Item** menu.*

Item	
Modify...	⌘M
Frame...	⌘B
Runaround...	⌘T
Duplicate	⌘D
Step and Repeat...	
Delete	⌘K
Group	⌘G
Ungroup	⌘U
Constrain	
Lock	**⌘L**
Send to Back	
Bring to Front	
Space/Align...	
Picture Box Shape	▶
Reshape Polygon	

Figure 7. *Select **Lock** from the **Item** menu.*

Item	
Modify...	⌘M
Frame...	⌘B
Runaround...	⌘T
Duplicate	⌘D
Step and Repeat...	
Delete	⌘K
Group	⌘G
Ungroup	⌘U
Constrain	
Unlock	**⌘L**
Send to Back	
Bring to Front	
Space/Align...	
Picture Box Shape	▶
Reshape Polygon	

Figure 8. *Select **Unlock** from the **Item** menu.*

About Locking:

Locking is a safety command that can be applied to any item — header, vertical rule, page number, etc. A locked item can only be moved or resized using the Measurements palette or a dialog box.

To lock an item:

1. Select the Item or Content tool.

2. Select an item to be locked.

3. Select Lock from the Item menu **(Figure 7)**.

To unlock an item:

1. Select the Item or Content tool.

2. Select an item to be unlocked.

3. Select Unlock from the Item menu **(Figure 8)**.

✔ Tips

■ When a locked item is selected with the Item tool, the cursor turns into a Padlock icon **(Figure 9)**.

■ The contents of a locked text box or picture box and the attributes of a line, such as style and width, can be edited.

■ Beware: a locked item **can** be deleted.

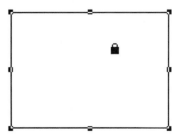

Figure 9. *The Padlock icon is displayed when a locked item is selected with the Item tool.*

To duplicate an item:

1. Select the Item tool.

2. Select a text box, picture box, group, or line to be duplicated **(Figure 10)**.

3. Select Duplicate from the Item menu **(Figures 11-12)**.

or

Hold down Command (⌘) and press "D".

✔ Tips

■ Duplicates are positioned according to the offsets last used in the Step and Repeat dialog box.

■ A linked text box cannot be duplicated.

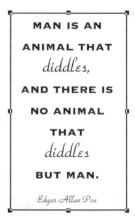

Figure 10. *Select an item to be duplicated.*

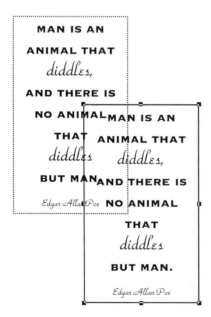

Figure 12. *A duplicate is made.*

Item	
Modify...	⌘M
Frame...	⌘B
Runaround...	⌘T
Duplicate	**⌘D**
Step and Repeat...	
Delete	⌘K
Group	⌘G
Ungroup	⌘U
Constrain	
Lock	⌘L
Send to Back	
Bring to Front	
Space/Align...	
Picture Box Shape	▶
Reshape Polygon	

Figure 11. *Select **Duplicate** from the **Item** menu.*

Figure 13. *Select an item.*

Figure 14. *The Step and Repeat dialog box.*

—— *The original item.*

Figure 15. *A Repeat Count of 3, Horizontal Offset of 0, and Vertical Offset of 5p5 was used to Step and Repeat this picture box.*

About Step and Repeat:

With the Step and Repeat command, multiple duplicates can be made at one time and the duplicates can be placed at a specified distance from each other.

To Step and Repeat an item:

1. Select the Item or Content tool.

2. Select a text box, picture box, group or line **(Figure 13)**.

3. Select Step and Repeat from the Item menu **(Figure 11)**.
   or
   Hold down Command (⌘) and Option and press "D".

4. Enter a number between 1 and 99 in the Repeat Count field for the number of duplicates to be made **(Figure 14)**.

5. Enter a number in the Horizontal Offset field. Enter a minus sign before the number to step and repeat items to the left of the original.

6. Enter a number in the Vertical Offset field. Enter a minus sign before the number to step and repeat items above the original.

7. Click OK or press Return **(Figure 15)**.

✔ Tips

■ If an alert prompt appears, reduce the repeat count and/or offset numbers so the duplicated items will fit within the limits of the pasteboard.

■ A linked text box cannot be duplicated with the Step and Repeat command.

Step and Repeat

To copy an item from one document to another:

1. Open two QuarkXPress files.

2. Resize both document windows so that they are side-by-side on the screen.

3. Select the Item tool.

4. Press and drag an item or group from one document window into the other. A duplicate is made automatically **(Figures 16-17)**.

✔ Tips

■ A linked text box cannot be duplicated with this method.

■ Items cannot be copied between documents in Thumbnails view.

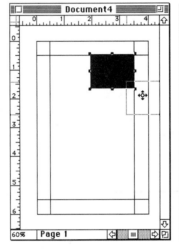
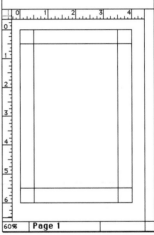

Figure 16. *Open two files, select the Item tool and press and drag an item from one file into the other.*

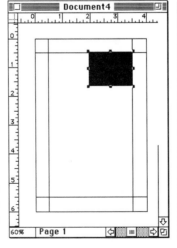
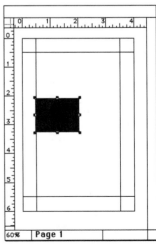

Figure 17. *A duplicate is made automatically as the item is dragged. The original item is unchanged.*

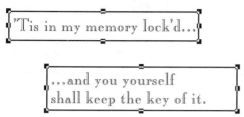

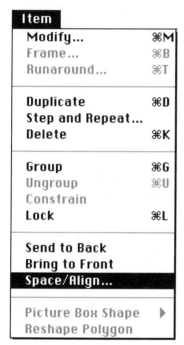

Figure 18. *Select two or more items.*

Figure 19. *Select **Space/Align** from the **Item** menu.*

To multiple-select items for aligning or distributing:

1. Select the Item tool.

2. Hold down Shift and click on each item to be multiple-selected.

or

Position the cursor outside the items to be multiple-selected, then press and drag a marquee around them.

To align items:

1. Multiple-select two or more items using the method outlined above **(Figure 18)**.

2. Select Space/Align from the Item menu **(Figure 19)**.

3. Check the Horizontal or Vertical box **(Figure 20)**.

4. Click the Space button.

5. Enter a positive or negative number between 0" and 10" in any measurement system in increments as small as 001. in the Space field to stair-step the items left or right if Horizontal is checked, up or down if Vertical is checked.

or

Enter 0 to align the items along their edges or centers.

6. Select an option from the Between pop-up menu.

7. Click Apply to preview.

8. Click OK or press Return **(Figure 21)**.

Align Items

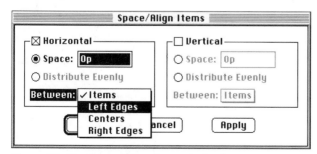

Figure 20. *The Space/Align Items dialog box.*

Figure 21. *Two text boxes are aligned along their left edges.*

To distribute items:

1. Multiple-select three or more items **(Figure 22)**.
   (See instructions on the previous page)

2. Select Space/Align from the Item menu **(Figure 19)**.

3. Check the Vertical or Horizontal box **(Figure 23)**.

4. Click Distribute Evenly.

5. Select an option from the Between pop-up menu.

6. Click Apply to preview.

7. Click OK or press Return **(Figure 24)**.

✔ Tip

■ The topmost and bottommost or leftmost and rightmost boxes remain stationary and the remaining items are distributed between them.

Figure 22. *Select three or more items.*

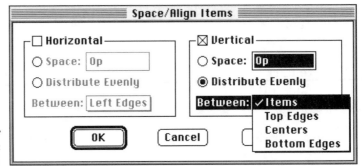

Figure 23. *The Space/Align Items dialog box.*

About multiple-selected items:

The position, number of columns, angle of rotation, background color, and other specifications can be modified for multiple-selected items. Modification options vary depending on whether the items are all text boxes, all picture boxes, all lines, or a combination thereof. Multiple-selected items can also be moved with the Item tool.

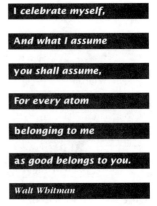

Figure 24. *These items are evenly distributed vertically.*

Figure 25. *A gray box in back of a black box is selected, as indicated by the eight handles.*

About Layering:

The most recently created item is automatically placed in front of all other items. The following commands can be used to change the stacking order.

To select an item that is behind another item:

1. Select the Item or Content tool.

2. Hold down Command (⌘), Option, Shift and click on an item. Each click will select the next item behind in succession **(Figure 25)**.

To send an item to the back or bring an item to the front:

1. Select the Item or Content tool.

2. Select an item.

3. Select Send to Back or Bring to Front from the Item menu **(Figures 26-27)**.

To send an item backward or bring an item forward:

1. Select the Item or Content tool.

2. Select an item.

3. Hold down Option and Select Send Backward or Bring Forward from the Item menu. This command will move an item backward or forward one layer at a time.

Item	
Modify...	⌘M
Frame...	⌘B
Runaround...	⌘T
Duplicate	⌘D
Step and Repeat...	
Delete	⌘K
Group	⌘G
Ungroup	⌘U
Constrain	
Lock	⌘L
Send to Back	
Bring to Front	
Space/Align...	
Picture Box Shape ▶	
Reshape Polygon	

Figure 26. *Select **Bring to Front** from the **Item** menu.*

Figure 27. *The gray box is now in front of the black box.*

Layer Items

About anchored boxes:

A text or picture box can be pasted into a text box as an inline graphic. It thereafter functions like a character, and remains anchored to the text. The contents of an anchored box can be edited. Lines and groups cannot be anchored.

To anchor a box:

1. Select the Item tool.
2. Select a text or picture box.
3. Select Copy or Cut from the Edit menu.
4. Select the Content tool.
5. Click in a text box to create an insertion point.
6. Select Paste from the Edit menu **(Figures 28-29)**.

To align an anchored box:

1. Select the Item or Content tool.
2. Select an anchored box.
3. Click the Ascent icon on the Measurements palette to align the top of the anchored box with the ascent of the character to its right **(Figure 30)**.
   or
   Click the Baseline icon to align the bottom of the anchored box with the baseline of the line of text it is anchored into.

To delete an anchored box:

1. Select the Content tool.
2. Click in the text box to the right of the anchored box. The cursor will be the height of the anchored box.
3. Press Delete.

✔ Tip

■ A box should not be anchored into text that is indented.

have mastery yet to chant the wonder at the wayside given to kings. Still by God's grace there surges within me singing magic grown to my life and power, how the wild bird portent hurled forth the Achaeans' twin-stemmed power single hearted, lords of the youth of Hellas, with spear and hand of strength to the land of Teucrus.

Aeschylus

Figure 28. *An anchored text box,* **Ascent** *aligned.*

Figure 29. *An anchored text box,* **Baseline** *aligned.*

*The **Ascent** icon on the Measurements palette.*

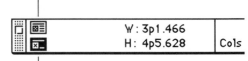

Figure 30. *The **Baseline** icon.*

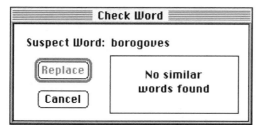

Figure 1. *Select* **Word** *from the* **Check Spelling** *pop-up menu.*

About Check Spelling:

A word, story or document can be checked for spelling accuracy. The QuarkXPress dictionary contains 120,000 words and cannot be edited. However, custom auxiliary dictionaries can be created to work in conjunction with the QuarkXPress dictionary.

To check the spelling of a word:

1. Select the Content tool.

2. Click or double-click a suspect word.

3. Select Word from the Check Spelling pop-up menu under the Utilities menu **(Figure 1)**.
   or
   Hold down Command (⌘) and press "W".

4. If the Suspect Word is not found in the QuarkXPress dictionary or any open auxiliary dictionary and no similar words are found, the Check Word dialog box will display "No similar words found." Click Cancel to exit the Check Word dialog box **(Figure 2)**.

If the Suspect Word and/or similar words are found in the QuarkXPress dictionary or any open auxiliary dictionary, they will be displayed. The Suspect Word, if found, will be highlighted. Double-click a replacement word; or highlight a word and click Replace; or click Cancel to leave the Suspect Word unchanged **(Figure 3)**.

Figure 2. *Neither the word "borogoves" nor similar words have been found in the QuarkXPress dictionary.*

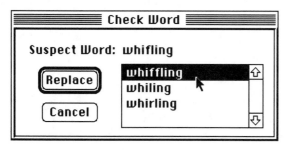

Figure 3. *Double-click a replacement word.*

About the Auxiliary Dictionary feature:

Custom auxiliary dictionaries can be created to work in conjunction with the QuarkXPress dictionary. Only one auxiliary dictionary can be open at a time, but a document can be checked for spelling several times, each time with a different auxiliary dictionary open. Unlike the QuarkXPress dictionary, auxiliary dictionaries can be edited.

To create an auxiliary dictionary:

1. Select Auxiliary Dictionary from the Utilities menu **(Figure 4)**.

2. Click New **(Figure 5)**.

3. Enter a name in the New Auxiliary Dictionary field **(Figure 6)**.

4. Select a location in which to save the dictionary, then click Save.

✔ Tip

■ If an auxiliary dictionary is created when no document is open, it will be the default auxiliary dictionary for all subsequently created documents.

To open an existing auxiliary dictionary:

1. Select Auxiliary Dictionary from the Utilities menu **(Figure 4)**.

2. Select an auxiliary dictionary **(Figure 5)**.

3. Click Open.

✔ Tip

■ The last auxiliary dictionary that is open when a document is saved will remain open until another auxiliary dictionary is opened for that document.

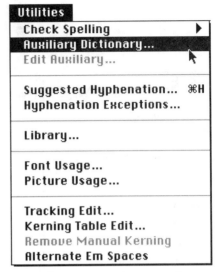

Figure 4. *Select **Auxiliary Dictionary** from the **Utilities** menu.*

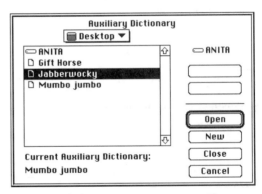

Figure 5. *Click **New** to create an auxiliary dictionary or select an existing auxiliary dictionary and click **Open**.*

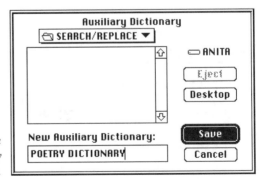

Figure 6. *Select a location in which to save the new auxiliary dictionary, then click **Save**.*

Check Spelling

Figure 7. *Select **Edit Auxiliary** from the **Utilities** menu.*

To edit an auxiliary dictionary:

1. Select Edit Auxiliary from the Utilities menu (**Figure 7**).

2. Type a new word in the entry field and click Add. No spaces or punctuation are permitted, and all characters are saved in lowercase (**Figure 8**).
or
Select a word and click Delete.

3. Click Save.

✔ Tips

■ A Suspect Word can also be added to an open auxiliary dictionary by clicking Keep in the Check Story or Check Document dialog box.

■ Words cannot actually be edited in the Edit Auxiliary Dictionary dialog box, they can only be deleted or added.

Figure 8. *This scroll list displays all the words in the Auxiliary Dictionary. To delete a word, select it and click **Delete**.*

*To add a new word, type a word in the entry field and click **Add**.*

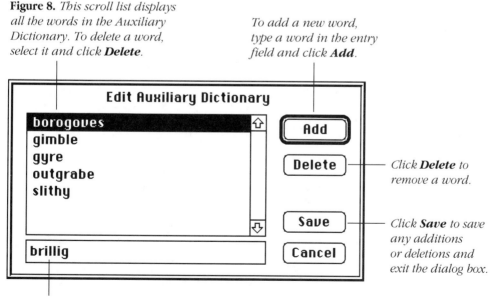

*Click **Delete** to remove a word.*

*Click **Save** to save any additions or deletions and exit the dialog box.*

Type a new word in the entry field.

To check the spelling of a story or document:

1. *Optional:* Open an auxiliary dictionary. *(See instructions on page 166)*

2. To Check Spelling in a **story**, select the Content tool and click in a story. Then select Story from the Check Spelling pop-up menu under the Utilities menu, or Hold down Command (⌘) and Option and press "W" **(Figure 9)**.

or

To Check Spelling in a **document**, select the Content tool and select Document from the Check Spelling pop-up menu under the Utilities menu. Spelling will automatically be checked from the beginning of the document.

3. When the Word Count box appears, click OK or press Return **(Figure 10)**.

4. Click Lookup to see a list of similar words. Double-click a similar word, or click a similar word and click Replace **(Figures 11-12)**.

or

Click Skip to skip over a word.

or

Click Keep to add a Suspect Word to the open auxiliary dictionary.

or

Type the correctly spelled word in the Replace with field and click Replace.

✔ Tips

■ After the spelling of a word is checked once, all other instances of the word are treated in the same manner.

■ Text cannot be edited manually in the document while the Check Story or Check Document dialog box is open.

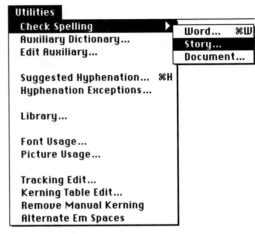

Figure 9. *Select **Story** or **Document** from the **Check Spelling** pop-up menu under the Utilities menu.*

Check Spelling

*The **Total** number
of words in the story.*

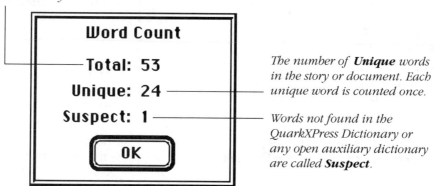

*The number of **Unique** words
in the story or document. Each
unique word is counted once.*

*Words not found in the
QuarkXPress Dictionary or
any open auxiliary dictionary
are called **Suspect**.*

Figure 10. *Click **OK** to proceed to the Check
Story or Check Document dialog box.*

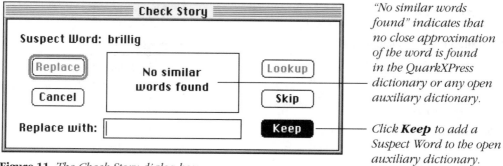

*"No similar words
found" indicates that
no close approximation
of the word is found
in the QuarkXPress
dictionary or any open
auxiliary dictionary.*

*Click **Keep** to add a
Suspect Word to the open
auxiliary dictionary.*

Figure 11. *The Check Story dialog box.*

*Double-click a suggested
word to substitute it for a
Suspect Word.*

Figure 12. *The Check Story dialog box.*

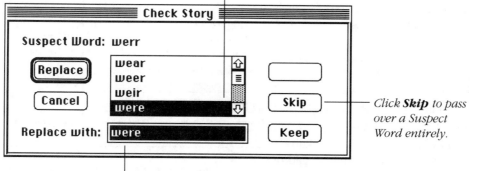

*Click **Skip** to pass
over a Suspect
Word entirely.*

*Or type a word in the **Replace with** field and click **Replace**.*

About Find/Change:

The Find/Change utility can be used to search for and replace text or attributes. The fields and check boxes on the left side of the Find/Change dialog box define the text or attributes to be searched for, and the fields and check boxes on the right side define what the text or attributes will be changed to.

To find and change spaces, characters, words, or attributes:

1. To search a story, select the Content tool and click in a story. To search a document, make sure no text boxes are selected.

2. Select Find/Change from the Edit menu **(Figure 13)**.
   or
   Hold down Command (⌘) and press "F".

3. Enter a maximum of 80 characters or spaces in the Find what field **(Figure 14)**.

4. Enter a maximum of 80 characters or spaces in the Change to field.
   or
   Leave the Change to field blank to delete the Find what text.

5. Check the Document box to search the whole document.

Steps 6 through 8 are optional.

6. Uncheck the Whole Word box to search for any instances of the Find what text that are embedded in a larger word.

7. Uncheck Ignore Case to search for only an exact match of the upper and lowercase configuration entered in the Find what field.

8. Uncheck the Ignore Attributes box to Find/Change attributes. Check the Font box or boxes to search for and/or

(Continued on the following page)

Figure 13. *Select **Find/Change** from the **Edit** menu.*

*Uncheck the **Ignore Attributes** box to expand the dialog box to Find/Change Font, Size, and Style attributes.*

Click the Zoom box to reduce the dialog box.

Figure 14.
The Find/Change dialog box.

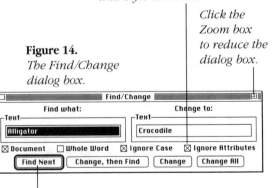

*Hold down Option to convert the **Find Next** button into the **Find First** button.*

**Enter these keystrokes
to Find/Change
non-printing characters.**

Character	Keystroke	Field will display
Tab	⌘ Tab	\t
New paragraph	⌘ Return	\p
New line	⌘ Shift-Return	\n
New column	⌘ Enter	\c
New box	⌘ Shift-Enter	\b
Current page #	⌘ 3	\3
Next box page #	⌘ 4	\4
Previous box page #	⌘ 2	\2
Wild card	⌘ ?	\?

change a font, then select a font from the pop-up menus **(Figure 15)**.

and/or

Check the Size box or boxes and enter a size or sizes.

and/or

In the Find what area, a checked Style will be found; an unchecked Style will not be found; a grayed style may or may not be found, but will not be changed.

In the Change to area, a checked Style will be applied to the text; an un-checked style will be removed from the text; a grayed style will be unchanged.

9. Hold down Option and click Find First to find the first instance in the document of the Find what text.
or
Click Find Next to find the next instance of the Find what text from your current location in the document.

10. Click Change, Then Find to change an instance and find the next instance.
or
Click Change to change one instance.
or
Click Change All to change all instances at once. A prompt will appear indicating the number of instances found.

11. Click the close box to exit Find/Change.

Find what area.   *Change to area.*

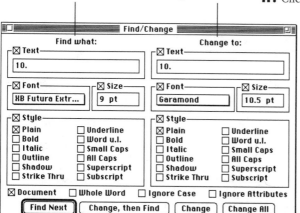

Figure 15. *Font, Size, and Style attributes can be included in a search when the Find/Change dialog box is expanded.*

✔ Tip

■ To display a list of fonts used in an active document, select Font Usage from the Utilities menu and press on the Font pop-up menu on the left side. This utility is useful for making a font list when sending a file to a service bureau **(Figures 16-17)**.

To use the Font Usage dialog box to search for and replace fonts, follow the instructions for Find/Change beginning on page 170.

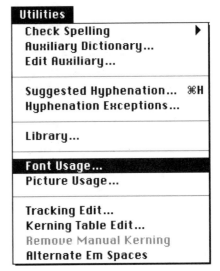

Figure 16. *Select **Font Usage** from the **Utilities** menu.*

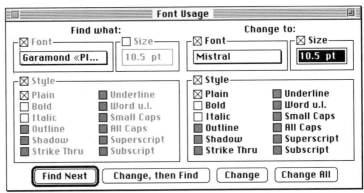

Figure 17. *The Font Usage dialog box.*

Figure 1.
*Select **Print**
from the
File menu.*

File	
New...	⌘N
Open...	⌘O
Close	
Save	⌘S
Save as...	
Revert to Saved	
Get Text/Picture...	⌘E
Save Text...	
Save Page as EPS...	
Document Setup...	
Page Setup...	
Print...	⌘P
Quit	⌘Q

To print a document:

1. Select Print from the File menu
(Figure 1).
or
Hold down Command (⌘) and
press "P".

2. Leave the default setting on All to
print all the document pages.
or
Enter numbers in the From and
To fields to print a range of pages
(Figure 2).

3. Click Print or press Return.
*(See also "To modify printer settings"
on the following page)*

*Enter the number of
Copies to be printed.
1 is the default.*

*Leave the default setting on **All** or enter
numbers in the **From** and **To** fields.
"End" can be entered in the To field.*

*Click **Print** or press
Return when you
are ready to print.*

*Click **Manual Feed**
for the printer to pause
between manual
paper feed insertions.*

*Click **Rough** to sup-
press picture printout.*

*Check the
Registration Marks
box to print crop
marks and registration
marks. The page size
should be smaller
than the paper size.*

LaserWriter "Lucky Pierre 2f" 7.0 [**Print**]
[Cancel]

Copies: 2   Pages: ○ All ● From: 4   To: end

Cover Page: ● No ○ First Page ○ Last Page

Paper Source: ● Paper Cassette ○ Manual Feed

Print: ○ Black & White ● Color/Grayscale

Destination: ● Printer ○ PostScript® File

Output: ● Normal ○ Rough ☐ Thumbnails
● All Pages ○ Odd Pages ○ Even Pages
☐ Back to Front ☐ Collate ☐ Spreads ☒ Blank Pages
☒ Registration Marks ● Centered ○ Off Center
OPI: [Include Images] ☒ Calibrated Output

Tiling: ● Off ○ Manual ○ Auto, overlap: 18p

Color: ☒ Make Separations Plate: [✓All Plates]
☐ Print Colors as Grays

Plate menu
✓All Plates
Black
Blue
Cyan
Green
Magenta
Red
Registration
Yellow

*Check the **Make Separations** box, then
make a selection from the Plate pop-up
menu to print a separate sheet of film or
paper for each color. To separate a color
TIFF picture, convert it to CMYK mode in
another application before importing it.*

*Click **Print
Colors as Grays**
to print gray simu-
lations of color.*

Figure 2. *The Print dialog box.*

To print pages that are larger than the printer's paper size:

An oversized document can be printed in sections on more than one sheet of paper using Auto or Manual Tiling. To print an oversized document on one sheet of paper, reduce the printout size **(Figure 4)**.

To print using Auto Tiling:

1. Select the appropriate Orientation icon in the Page Setup dialog box, opened from the File menu **(Figure 4)**.

2. Select Print from the File menu.

3. Check the Auto Tiling box **(Figure 2)**.

4. Enter a number in the Auto, overlap field.

5. Click Print.

To modify printer settings:

1. Select Page Setup from the File menu.

2. Make any desired modifications **(Figure 4)**.

3. Click OK or press Return.

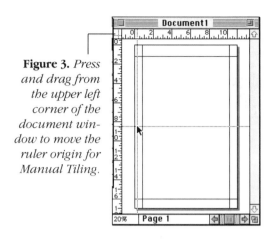

Figure 3. *Press and drag from the upper left corner of the document window to move the ruler origin for Manual Tiling.*

To print an 11" x 17" page on two sheets of paper.

Check the landscape Orientation icon in the Page Setup dialog box **(Figure 4)**. Print the page with the Tiling box unchecked. Then press and drag the ruler origin to 8.5" on the vertical ruler to move the position from which the document will begin printing **(Figure 3)**, and Print again with the Manual Tiling box checked **(Figure 2)**.

Figure 4. *The **Page Setup** dialog box.*

*Click one of the **Paper** size buttons.*

*Enter a number between 25% and 400% to **Reduce** or **Enlarge** the printout size.*

*Click an **Orientation** icon to print a document in portrait or landscape format.*

*Select a printer from the **Printer Type** pop-up menu.*

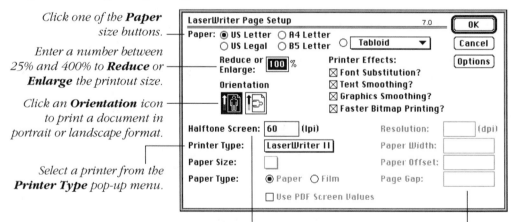

*Enter an lpi (lines per inch) setting between 15 and 400 in the **Halftone Screen** field. A setting between 65 and 85 is usually required by newspapers; a setting between 120 and 150 is used for magazines; books require higher settings. A setting of 60 is recommended for printing to a Laserwriter.*

These dimmed fields are available when an imagesetter is selected from the Printer Type pop-up menu.

Printing

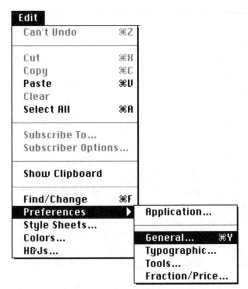

Figure 1. *Select **Application, General, Typographic, Tools,** or **Fraction/Price** (if available) from the **Preferences** pop-up menu under the **Edit** menu.*

About defaults:

Default settings are the values that automatically apply when a feature or tool is used. For example, when the Line tool is used, a line is automatically drawn in a particular width. That width is the default setting. Default settings can be customized.

Select Application from the Preferences pop-up menu under the Edit menu to customize defaults for all documents in the QuarkXPress application. For example, the Page Grabber Hand is available in all documents when turned on in Application Preferences **(Figure 1)**.

Select General, Typographic, Tools or Fraction/Price (with the FeaturesPlus XTension) without a document open to set application-wide defaults; select from within an active document to set defaults for that document only.

Defaults for Style Sheets, Colors, H&Js, and Auxiliary Dictionaries are set in their own individual dialog boxes. For example, a style sheet created with no document open will appear in all subsequently created documents.

Instructions for setting defaults are also outlined in other chapters.

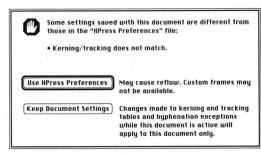

Figure 2. *The XPress Preferences prompt.*

About XPress Preferences.

Information about tracking and kerning tables, hyphenation exceptions, and custom frames is stored in individual documents and in the QuarkXPress folder in a file called XPress Preferences. If, upon opening a file, the document settings do not match the XPress Preferences settings, a prompt will appear. Click Use XPress Preferences or Keep Document Settings **(Figure 2)**.

Key to the General Preferences dialog box:

1-2 The default Horizontal and Vertical Measures are set separately. Select Inches, Inches Decimal, Picas, Points, Millimeters, Centimeters, or Ciceros. *(See page 16)*

3 With Auto Page Insertion, pages will be added at End of Story, End of Section, End of Document, or not at all (Off). *(See pages 51-53)*

4 Framing can be applied to the Inside or Outside edges of a box.

5 Ruler Guides can be set to display In Front of or Behind page elements. *(See page 99)*

6 The Master Page Items options, Keep Changes and Delete Changes, affect whether modified items from the previous master page are kept or deleted when a new master page is applied to a document page. *(See page 138)*

7 Auto Picture Import options include Off, On, and On (verify). *(See page 119)*

8 With Greek Pictures checked, pictures are displayed only when selected. Otherwise, they display as solid gray boxes. Greeking speeds up screen redraw.

9 Greek Below indicates the point size below which text displays as solid gray bars.

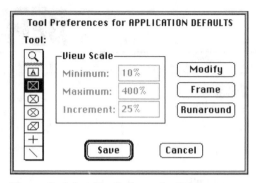

Figure 3. *Select* **Tools** *from the Preferences pop-up menu under the Edit menu, or double-click any of the Item creation tools or the Zoom tool to open the* **Tool Preferences** *dialog box. Click* **Modify, Frame,** *or* **Runaround** *to modify default settings.*

Figure 4. *Ligatures. A ligature is a pair or series of characters that is kerned so tightly they appear to be joined. Select* **Typographic Preferences** *from the* **Edit** *menu to turn the Ligatures option on or off. Other defaults in the Typographic Preferences dialog box include Superior, Subscript, Small Caps, Superior scaling and position values, and Auto Kern Above to set the point size above which character pairs are kerned automatically.*

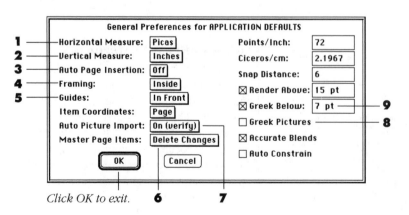

Click OK to exit.

Figure 5. *Options on the left side of the* **General Preferences** *dialog box are selected from pop-up menus.*

Set Defaults

Glossary

Ascender	The part of a lowercase letter that extends above the x-height, as in the letters *b, d, f, h* and *l*.
Baseline	The invisible line on which most uppercase and lower-case letters sit.
Baseline Shift	Raise or lower one or more characters above or below the baseline.
Bleed	An item that extends beyond the edge of the page.
Condense Type	Make characters narrower than normal.
Descender	The part of a lowercase letter that extends below the baseline, as in the letters *p* and *j*.
Em Space	The width occupied by two zeros in a given font.
En Space	The width occupied by one zero in a given font.
EPS	Encapsulated Postscript, a picture file format.
Extend Type	Make characters wider than normal.
File	An electronic document. A QuarkXPress file can consist of one or more pages.
Folio	Page number.
Hanging Indent	A format in which the first line of a paragraph is aligned flush left and the remaining lines are indented.
Horizontal Scale	Character width.
Imagesetter	A high resolution printer.
Kern	Adjust the space between two characters.
Leading	The space measured from baseline to baseline between lines of type.
Line	A line of type, *or,* a line that is drawn with a Line tool.
Link	To connect text boxes into a chain so that text flows continuously from one box into another.
Orphan	The first line of a paragraph that falls at the bottom of a column.
Pica	A unit of measure used in graphic arts. Six picas equals 1 inch; 1 pica equals 12 points.

Paragraph	Any number of characters followed by a Return.
Point	The unit used to measure type size, leading and rules. In the example "2p8," the numbers before the p indicate picas and the numbers after the "p" indicate points.
Polygon	A closed shape composed of three or more straight sides.
Resolution	The degree of sharpness of detail that a printer can achieve (dots per inch).
Rule	A line that is anchored to text using the Paragraph Rules feature.
Ruler Origin	The intersection of the horizontal and vertical rulers, usually positioned at the upper left corner of the page.
Sans Serif Font	A font with no finishing strokes projecting from the ends of its characters.
Serif Font	A font with short finishing strokes projecting from the ends of its characters.
Spread	Two or more pages displayed or printed side-by-side.
Story	Text that is contained in one box or a series of linked boxes. A document can contain more than one story.
TIFF	A picture file format used for saving scanned images (Tag Image File Format).
Track	Adjust the space to the right of one or more highlighted characters.
Typeface	A distinctive type design, such as Optima. The Optima typeface includes the Optima Regular, Optima Oblique, and Optima Bold fonts.
Widow	The last line of a paragraph that falls at the top of a column.
X-height	The height of the lowercase "x" in a particular font.

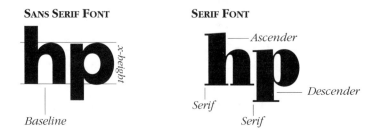

SANS SERIF FONT   SERIF FONT

List of Keyboard Shortcuts by Chapter

Key

ᐟ Click

ᐟᐟ   Double-click

----ᐟ   Press and drag

Chapter 1: **The Basics**

Tool palette

Show Tools or select next tool	⌘ Tab
Show Tools or select previous tool	⌘ Shift Tab
Keep a tool selected	Option click on tool
Tool preferences...	ᐟᐟ Item creation or Zoom tool
Move item with Item tool not selected	Hold down ⌘
About QuarkXPress (Help)	⌘ ? or ⌘ /

Measurements palette

Display Measurements palette/ highlight first field	⌘ Option M
Highlight field	ᐟᐟ
Highlight next field	Tab
Highlight previous field	Shift Tab
Cancel/Exit	⌘ Period
Apply/Exit	Enter or Return
Revert to original values	⌘ Z

Dialog boxes

OK (or heavy bordered button)	Return
Cancel	⌘ Period
Apply	⌘ A
Continuous Apply	⌘ Option A or Option ᐟ Apply
Yes	⌘ Y
No	⌘ N
Highlight field	ᐟᐟ
Highlight next field	Tab
Highlight previous field	Shift Tab
Revert to original values	⌘ Z

Rulers

Show/Hide Rulers	⌘ R

Chapter 3: **Create a Document**

New...	⌘ N
Open...	⌘ O
Save	⌘ S
Save As...	⌘ Option S

Keyboard Shortcuts

Quit	⌘ Q
Close all document windows	Option ⬉ Close box

Chapter 4: **Getting Around**

Change view sizes

Fit in Window view	⌘ Zero
Page/spread and pasteboard	Option Fit in Window view
Actual Size view	⌘ 1
Enlarge view size	Control ⬉ or Control ⬉
Reduce view size	Control Option ⬉

Move through a document

Go To...	⌘ J
Start of document	Control A or Home
End of document	Control D or End
Scroll up one screen	Control K or Page Up
Scroll down one screen	Control L or Page Down
Scroll to first page	Control Shift A or Shift Home
Scroll to last page	Control Shift D or Shift End
Scroll to previous page	Control Shift K or Shift Page Up
Scroll to next page	Control Shift L or Shift Page Down
Page Grabber Hand	Option ⬉

Chapter 5: **Text Input**

Show/Hide Invisibles	⌘ I

Highlight Text

One word	⬉⬉
One line	⬉⬉⬉
One paragraph	⬉⬉⬉⬉
Entire story (Select All)	⬉⬉⬉⬉⬉ or ⌘ A

Move the cursor

(Hold down Shift to highlight while moving.)

Character-by-character	Left & Right Arrows
Line-by-line	Up & Down Arrows
Word-by-word	⌘ Left & Right Arrows
Paragraph-by-paragraph	⌘ Up & Down Arrows
Start of line	⌘ Option Left Arrow
End of line	⌘ Option Right Arrow
Start of story	⌘ Option Up Arrow
End of story	⌘ Option Down Arrow

The Clipboard

Cut	⌘ X
Copy	⌘ C
Paste	⌘ V

Text Boxes

Frame...	⌘ B
Modify... (Item Specifications)	⌘ M
Delete box	⌘ K

Chapter 6: **Text Flow**

Get text...	⌘ E
Current text box page number	⌘ 3
Previous text box page number	⌘ 2
Next text box page number	⌘ 4

Chapter 7: **Paragraph Formats**

Formats...	⌘ Shift F
Leading...	⌘ Shift E
Tabs...	⌘ Shift T
Rules...	⌘ Shift N
Increase leading 1 point	⌘ Shift "
Decrease leading 1 point	⌘ Shift :
Increase leading 1/10 point	⌘ Option Shift "
Decrease leading 1/10 point	⌘ Option Shift :
Indent Here character	⌘ \
Delete all tab stops	Option ⭠ tabs ruler
Right-Indent tab	Option Tab
Suggested Hyphenation	⌘ H

Chapter 8: **Typography**

Character...	⌘ Shift D
Display Measurements palette/ highlight Font field	⌘ Option Shift M
Increase Horizontal Scaling 5%	⌘]
Decrease Horizontal Scaling 5%	⌘ [
Baseline Shift up 1 point	⌘ Option Shift +
Baseline Shift down 1 point	⌘ Option Shift Hyphen

Resize text

Increase point size to preset sizes	⌘ Shift >
Decrease point size to preset sizes	⌘ Shift <
Increase point size by 1 point	⌘ Option Shift >
Decrease point size by 1 point	⌘ Option Shift <
Other size...	⌘ Shift \

Style text

Plain text	⌘ Shift P
Bold	⌘ Shift B
Italic	⌘ Shift I
Underline	⌘ Shift U
Word Underline	⌘ Shift W

Keyboard Shortcuts

Strike Thru	⌘ Shift /
Outline	⌘ Shift O
Shadow	⌘ Shift S
All Caps	⌘ Shift K
Small Caps	⌘ Shift H
Superscript	⌘ Shift +
Subscript	⌘ Shift Hyphen
Superior	⌘ Shift V

Horizontal alignment

Left alignment	⌘ Shift L
Right alignment	⌘ Shift R
Center alignment	⌘ Shift C
Justified alignment	⌘ Shift J

Tracking and kerning

Increase Kerning/Tracking 10 units	⌘ Shift }
Decrease Kerning/Tracking 10 units	⌘ Shift {
Increase Kerning/Tracking 1 unit	⌘ Option Shift }
Decrease Kerning/Tracking 1 unit	⌘ Option Shift {

Word space tracking

For use only with FeaturesPlus XTension.

Increase Word Space 10 units	⌘ Shift Control }
Decrease Word Space 10 units	⌘ Shift Control {
Increase Word Space 1 unit	⌘ Option Shift Control }
Decrease Word Space 1 unit	⌘ Option Shift Control {

Special characters

Insert one Zapf Dingbats character	⌘ Shift Z
Insert one Symbol character	⌘ Shift Q
New paragraph	Return
New line	Shift Return
Discretionary new line	⌘ Return
Discretionary hyphen	⌘ Hyphen
Nonbreaking standard hyphen	⌘ =
Nonbreaking standard space	⌘ Space bar
New column	Enter
New box	Shift Enter
Breaking en space	Option Space bar
Nonbreaking en space	⌘ Option Space bar
Breaking flex space	Option Shift Space bar
Nonbreaking flex space	⌘ Option Shift Space bar
Nonbreaking em dash	⌘ Option =
Breaking em dash	Option Shift Hyphen
Nonbreaking en dash	Option Hyphen

Chapter 9: **Pictures**

Import a picture

Get Picture...	⌘ E

In Get Picture dialog box:

Import picture at 72 dpi if Low Resolution Tiff is checked in Application Preferences dialog box	Shift Open
Import picture at 36 dpi if Low Resolution Tiff is unchecked in Application Preferences dialog box	Shift Open
TIFF line art to grayscale	Option Open
TIFF grayscale to line art	⌘ Open
TIFF color to grayscale	⌘ Open

Pictures and picture boxes

Center picture in box	⌘ Shift M
Frame...	⌘ B
Modify... (Item Specifications)	⌘ M
Delete box	⌘ K
Move picture in box 1 point	Arrow keys
Move picture in box ⅒ point	Option Arrow keys
Fit picture to box	⌘ Shift F
Fit picture to box (maintain aspect ratio)	⌘ Option Shift F
Enlarge picture in 5% increments	⌘ Option Shift >
Reduce picture in 5% increments	⌘ Option Shift <
Constrain box to square or circle	Shift ····➤
Resize box (maintain aspect ratio)	Option Shift ····➤
Scale picture and box	⌘ ····➤
Scale picture and box (maintain aspect ratio)	⌘ Option Shift ····➤

Style a picture

Other Contrast...	⌘ Shift C
Other Screen...	⌘ Shift S
Negative	⌘ Shift Hyphen
Normal contrast	⌘ Shift N
High contrast	⌘ Shift H
Posterized contrast	⌘ Shift P

Text wrap

Runaround...	⌘ T

Modify a polygon picture box or Runaround polygon

Create a handle	⌘ ➤ on line segment
Delete a handle	⌘ ➤ on handle
Constrain line or handle movement to 0°, 45°, 90°	Shift ····➤
Temporarily suspend text reflow	Space bar
Delete Runaround polygon	⌘ Shift ➤

Chapter 10: **Lines**

Increase width in preset range	⌘ Shift >
Decrease width in preset range	⌘ Shift <
Increase width by 1 point	⌘ Option Shift >
Decrease width by 1 point	⌘ Option Shift <
Other width	⌘ Shift \
Constrain resizing/rotating to 0°/45°/90°	Shift ⌇➤
Constrain to same angle	Option Shift ⌇➤

Chapter 11: **Style Sheets**

Style Sheets...	⌘ ➤ style sheet name in Style Sheets palette
Apply No Style, then style sheet	Option ➤ style sheet name in Style Sheets palette

Chapter 12: **Master Pages**

Automatic page numbering command	⌘ 3

Chapter 13: **Color**

Colors...	⌘ ➤ color in Colors palette

Chapter 15: **Multiple Items**

Group	⌘ G
Ungroup	⌘ U
Lock/Unlock	⌘ L
Duplicate	⌘ D
Step and Repeat...	⌘ Option D
Select through layers	⌘ Option Shift ➤
Bring Forward one level	Option Item menu
Send Backward one level	Option Item menu
Move item 1 point	Arrow keys
Move item 1/10 point	Option Arrow keys

Chapter 16: **Search & Replace**

Check Spelling: Word...	⌘ W
Check Spelling: Story...	⌘ Option W
Find/Change...	⌘ F
Change Find Next button to Find First	Option (in Find/Change dialog box)

Chapter 17: **Printing**

Page Setup...	⌘ Option P
Print...	⌘ P
Print Status	Shift Print

Chapter 18: **Default Settings**

General Preferences...	⌘ Y
Typographic Preferences...	⌘ Option Y

Index

A

Align items, 161
Alignment, of text
    horizontal, 88
    vertical, 67, 89
Anchored boxes, 164
Anchored rules, 80-82, 130
Append,
    colors, 144, 153
    style sheets, 52, 132-133, 153
Application Preferences, 31, 175
Applications menu, 19
Arrows, line endcaps, 122
Auto Image, Runaround setting, 112-113, 115
Auto Page Insertion, 51-53, 57, 176
Auto Picture Import, 119, 176
Automatic Page Numbering, 136
Automatic Text Box, 20-21, 51-52, 54,
    137, 139
Auxiliary Dictionaries, 165-169
    create, 166
    edit, 167
    open, 166

B

Background, of box,
    apply color to, 147
    linear blend, 148
    make transparent, 46, 118
Balloon Help, 2-3, 16
Baseline Shift, 93
Bleed, create, 98
Blends, linear, 147-148
Boxes, picture,
    about, 17-18
    anchored, 164
    color, 147
    convert shape, 104, 108
    corner radius, 104
    create, 95
    delete, 97
    frame, 107
    layer, 118, 163
    move, 97-98
    polygon, 108-109
    position using guides, 99
    resize, 96

rotate, 105
    wrap text around, 114
Boxes, text,
    about, 17-18
    anchored, 164
    automatic, 3, 20-21, 51-52, 54, 137, 139
    color, 147
    columns, 49
    copy, 41
    create, 35
    delete, 37, 61
    duplicate, 158
    frame, 42-43
    inset, 38, 44, 65, 67
    layer, 46-47, 163
    link, 59
    make transparent, 46, 118
    move, 37
    position using guides, 99
    resize, 36
    rotate, 45
    unlink, 60-61
    wrap text around, 48
Bring Forward command, 163
Bring to Front command, 46, 114, 163

C

Character dialog box, 86
Check Spelling, 165-169
    a story or document, 168-169
    a word, 165
Clear command, 37
Clipboard, 40-41
Close a file, 28
Close box, 2-3
Color, 141-148
    about, 141
    append, 144, 153
    apply to a frame, 42-43, 145
    apply to a line, 122, 146
    apply to a picture, 146
    apply to background of a box, 147
    apply to text, 145
    CMYK, 141, 143-144, 146
    default, 143
    delete, 144

edit, 144
Focoltone, 143
linear blend, 147-148
Pantone, 141-142
process, 141, 143-144
separations, printing, 141-143, 146, 173
spot, 141-142
Trumatch, 143
Colors palette, 145-148
Columns,
modify column guides, 139
modify the number of, 49
specify for new document, 20-21
Condense type, 92
Contents, and Content tool, 17
Continued from/continued on jump lines, 62
Contrast, modify for grayscale picture, 111
Convert picture box shape, 104, 108
Convert Quotes when importing text, 52
Copy,
items, document to document, 160
onto Clipboard, 40-41
pages, document to document, 58, 138
paragraph formats, 70
Corner radius of picture box, 104
Crop a picture, 103
Crop marks, print with, 173
Current Page Number, 136
Current page number indicator, 2-3
Cut onto Clipboard, 40-41

D
Defaults, set 175-176
auxiliary dictionary, 166
colors, 143
style sheets, 84, 130, 134
Delete,
a picture, 103
a picture box, 97
a polygon, 108
a Runaround polygon, 116
a text box, 37, 61
an item from a group, 156
pages, 57, 136
text, 40
Dialog boxes, how to use, 10-11
Dictionary, see Auxiliary Dictionaries
Display, pop-up menu, 138
Distribute items, 162

Document Layout Palette,
about, 14
master pages, 135-139
section starts, 140
use to delete pages, 57
use to insert pages, 55-56
use to move through a document, 33
use to rearrange pages, 58
Document Setup dialog box, 26
Drop Caps, automatic, 73-74
Duplicate,
a file using Save As, 25
an item, 158
items between documents, 160
pages between documents, 58, 138

E
Edit menu, 6
Endcaps, line, 122
EPS, Save Page As, 112-113
Export text using Save Text command, 50
Extend type, 92
Extended keyboard, use to move
through a document, 32

F
Facing-page document,
about, 135
add pages to, 55-56
convert to single-sided, 26
create new, 20-21
Document Layout palette for a, 14
master pages, 137-138
File,
create a new, 20-21
close, 28
duplicate, 25
menu, 6
open, 27
save, 22-24, 28
Find/Change, 170-171
Finder, 19
First Baseline, 38, 67
Font Usage, 172
Fonts, change, 86, 172
Formats, see Paragraph Formatting
Frame,
a picture box, 107
a text box, 42-43

color, 42-43, 107, 145
set default for, 176

G

General Preferences, 51, 99, 119, 138, 175-176
Get Picture, to import a picture, 100
Get Text, to import text, 52
Glossary, Appendix A, 177
Go To command, 32, 54
Greek Below, 176
Greek Pictures, 176
Group/Ungroup command, 155-156
Guides, modify column, margin, 49, 139
Guides, ruler,
    position items using, 99
    set default measurement system for, 176
Gutter width,
    modify, 49
    specify for new document, 20-21

H

H&Js, 83-84
Hanging indents, 71-72
Horizontal alignment of text, 88
Horizontal Scale command, 92
Hyphenation, 83-84

I

Import,
    a picture, 100
    text, 51-53
Indent Here character, 72
Indents,
    first line, 65, 77
    hanging, 71-72
    Indent Here character, 72
    left and right, 63-64, 77
Input text, 38
Insert pages, 54-56, 136
Inset, Text, 38, 44, 65, 67
Invisible characters, 38, 72, 75, 171
Item menu, 8
Items and the Item tool, 17-18

J

Jump Lines, create, 62
Justification,
    horizontal, 88
    vertical, 89

K

Keep Document Settings, 175
Keep Lines Together command, 69
Keep with Next ¶ command, 69
Kerning,
    next to a drop cap, 74
    remove manual, command, 91
    text, 90-91
Key Caps, 94
Keyboard shortcuts,
    how to perform, 15
    list of, Appendix B, 179

L

Launch QuarkXPress, 19
Layer,
    items, 163
    picture behind text, 118
    text boxes, 46-47
Leading, 66-67
Library, 149-154
    about, 149
    add an entry to, 151-152
    append style sheet from, 132, 153
    create, 149
    delete an entry from, 151
    label an entry, 154
    open, 150
    retrieve an entry from, 153
Ligatures, 176
Line break commands, 70, 75
Linear blends, create, 147-148
Lines, 121-124
    about, 121
    color, 122, 146
    draw, 121
    move, 124
    resize, 123
    style, 122
    width, 122
Linking,
    automatic, 53-54
    manual, 59
Lock command, 157

M

Manual Image Runaround setting, 112, 116-117
Margins,
    guides, 2-3

modify margin guides, 139
set for new document, 20-21
Master Pages, 135-140
    about, 135
    append, 138
    apply, 55, 138
    copy master items, 139
    create, 137
    modify, 137
    modify margin and column guides, 139
    page numbering on, 136
    rename, 137
    remove from facing-page document, 26
    select for inserted pages, 54
    set default for applying, 138, 176
Measurement systems,
    abbreviations, 16, 36
    default, 16, 36, 176
Measurements palette, 2-3, 13, 18
Menu bar, 2-3
Menus,
    Edit, 6
    File, 6
    how to use, 5
    Item, 8
    Page, 8
    Style, 7
    Utilities, 9
    View, 9
Mouse, how to use, 4
Move,
    a line, 124
    a picture box, 97-98
    a text box, 37
    command, to rearrange pages, 58
    through a document, 31-33
Multiple-select items, 155, 161-162

N

New file,
    create, 20-21
    save, 22-23, 28
Next Box Page Number, 62
Normal style sheet, 84, 130, 134
Numbering,
    current page number indicator, 2-3
    jump lines, 62
    pages, 136
    sections, 32-33, 140

O

Open a file, 27
Orientation, page, for printing, 20, 174
Orphan control, 69
Overflow, text, 38, 53

P

Page boundary, 2-3
Page Grabber Hand, 31, 175
Page menu, 8
Page Setup, printer, 20, 174
Page size,
    modify, 26
    specify for a new file, 20-21
Pages,
    copy from one document to another,
        58, 138
    delete, 57, 136
    insert, 54-56, 136
    number, 136
    rearrange, 58
    section numbering, 32-33, 140
Paragraph formatting, 63-84
    about, 63
    add space between paragraphs, 68
    copy formats from one paragraph
        to another, 70
    create a new, 38
    drop caps, automatic, 73-74
    hanging indents, 71-72
    horizontal alignment, 88
    hyphenation, 83-84
    indents, 63-65, 71-72
    insert line break, 70, 75
    keep lines together, 69
    leading, 66-67
    orphan/widow control, 69
    rules, 80-82, 130
    space before/after, 68
    tabs, 65, 75-79
    using style sheets, 125-127, 130-131
Paragraph rules, 80-82, 130
Paste from Clipboard, 40-41
Pasteboard, 2-3, 26, 98
Picture Boxes, see Boxes, picture
Picture Usage, 120, 153
Pictures, 95-120
    about, 95
    apply color to, 146

color separate, 146, 173
contrast setting, 111
crop, 103
delete, 103
Greek, 176
import, 95, 100
layer behind text, 118
posterize, 110
resize, 101-102
rotate, 105-106
shade, apply, 110
style, 110-111
update, 119-120
wrap text around, 112-117
Polygon picture box, 108-109
Polygon, Runaround, 116-117
Posterize a picture, 110
Preferences,
    Application, 31, 175
    General, 51, 99, 119, 138, 175-176
    Tool, 175-176
    Typographic, 84, 175-176
    XPress, 175
Previous Box Page Number, 62
Printing, 20, 173-174
    bleed, 98
    crop marks, 173
    oversized documents, 174

Q

Quit the application, 28
Quotes,
    convert to "curly," 52
    input "curly," 94

R

Rearrange pages, 58
Registration marks, print, 173
Remove Manual Kerning, 91
Resize,
    a line, 123
    a picture, 101-102
    a picture box, 96
    a text box, 36
    type, 85
Resize box, 2-3
Reverse paragraph rules, 82
Reverse type, 145, 147
Revert to Saved, 24, 55

Rotate,
    a line, 121, 123
    a picture, 105-106
    a picture and box, 105
    a text box, 45
Ruler Guides, 2-3, 99, 176
Ruler Origin, 2-3, 174
Rulers, 2-3, 176
Rules, Paragraph, 80-82, 130
Runaround,
    Auto Image, 112-113, 115
    Item, 48, 114
    Manual Image, 112, 116-117
    None, 46, 116

S

Save,
    a new file, 22-24, 28
    an existing file, 24, 28
Save As, to duplicate a file, 25
Save Page as EPS, 112-113
Save Text command, to export, 50
Scale, Horizontal, command, 92
Scroll arrows, bars, boxes, 31
Search and replace,
    characters and/or attributes, 170-171
    fonts only, 172
Section,
    create, 140
    display pages of using Go To command, 32
    Document Layout palette, 33, 140
Select All command, 39
Send Backward command, 163
Send to Back command, 163
Shade,
    a frame, 42-43, 107, 145
    a line, 122, 146
    a picture, 110, 146
    background, 147
    text, 145
Shift, Baseline, 93
Shortcuts, keyboard, Appendix B, 179
Show Document Layout, see Document
    Layout palette
Show Invisibles, 38, 72, 75
Show Style Sheets, 128
Single-sided documents, 14, 56, 135
Snap to Guides, 99
Space/Align feature, 161-162

Space Before/Space After commands, 68
Special characters, insert, 94
Spelling, Check, 165-169
　　auxiliary dictionary, 165-169
　　story or document, 168-169
　　word, 165
Spread, create a, 56
Step and Repeat, 159
Style a picture, 110-111
Style menu, 7
Style Sheets, 125-134
　　about, 125
　　append, 52, 132-133, 153
　　apply, 128
　　Based On, 129
　　create, 126-127
　　default, 130, 175
　　delete, 134
　　duplicate, 134
　　edit, 130-131
　　Normal, 84, 130, 134
Style text, 87
Suppress Printout, 123

T

Tabs, 75-79
　　about, 75
　　insert into text, 75
　　move custom tab stops, 65, 76
　　remove custom tab stops, 65, 79
　　set custom tab stops, 65, 76-78
　　style sheets, 126-127, 130-131
Template, create a, 23
Text,
　　baseline shift, 93
　　color, 145
　　delete, 40
　　fonts, change, 86, 172
　　format using style sheets, 125-129
　　Greek, 176
　　highlight, 39
　　horizontal alignment, 88
　　horizontal scale, 92
　　hyphenation, 83-84
　　import, 51-53
　　input, 38
　　inset, 38, 44, 65, 67
　　kerning, 90-91
　　leading, 66-67
　　rearrange using Clipboard, 41
　　resize, 85

Save Text command, to export, 50
　　shade, 145
　　style, 87
　　tracking, 90-91
　　vertical alignment, modify, 67, 89
　　wrap, around a picture, 115-117
　　wrap, around a picture box, 114
　　wrap, around another text box, 48
Text boxes, see Boxes, text
Text Inset, 38, 44, 65, 67
Text Overflow symbol, 38, 53
Thumbnails view,
　　copy pages in, 58
　　rearrange pages in, 58
　　select, 29
Tiling, print option, 174
Title bar, 2-3
Tool palette, 2-3, 12
Tool Preferences, 176
Tracking, 90-91
Transparent, make a text box, 46, 118
Type, see Text
Typeface, see Fonts
Typographic Preferences, 84, 175-176

U

Ungroup command, 156
Unlink text boxes, 60-61
Update a picture, 119-120
Use XPress Preferences, 175
Utilities menu, 9

V

Vertical Alignment of type, 67, 89
View,
　　sizes, 29-30
　　Thumbnails, 29, 58
　　View Percent field, 2-3, 29
　　View menu, 9, 29

W

Widow control, 69
Word space tracking, 91

X

XPress Preferences, 175

Z

Zapf Dingbat, insert one, 94
Zoom box, 2-3
Zoom tool, access using keyboard, 30